Coupleship

How to Build a Relationship

Sharon Wegscheider-Cruse

Illustrations by Kathleen Johnson

Health Communications, Inc.
Deerfield Beach, Florida

Sharon Wegscheider-Cruse
Onsite Training & Consulting, Inc.
2820 West Main
Rapid City, SD 57702

Library of Congress Cataloging-in-Publication Data

Wegscheider-Cruse, Sharon, 1938—
    Coupleship: how to have a relationship / Sharon
    Wegscheider-Cruse.
        p.   cm.
    Bibliography: p.
    ISBN 0-932194-64-8
        1. Marriage.   2. Interpersonal relations.   3. Intimacy
    (Psychology)   I.   Title.
    HQ734.W436   1988   87-30877
    646.7'8 — dc 19   CIP

Cover design by Vicki Sommer

Published by Health Communications, Inc.
Deerfield Beach, Florida 33069

Dedication

To my husband, Joe Cruse, who remains my
best friend and spiritual soulmate. I love you . . .

Special thanks to Mark Worden and his gifted
contribution to this book.

For once, someone was able to help us take an honest look at our relationship. We can see the positives and the negatives and have been given tools to use to make our coupleship a truly intimate one. In a safe, loving environment, taking off our masks gave us the freedom to grow.

Martha Eames, M.D.
Bruce Eames, M.D.

In the five years that we have known Sharon, she has been our professional mentor. We have learned much from her, but she has never attempted to present herself as a guru. More significantly, she has been our guide as we redirected our lives, and this has truly been a spiritual process. Always she is human, real, openly expressive, and easy to understand: and in this lies the value of her writing. The wide recognition of co-dependency as an illness is due to Sharon's efforts.

Cheryl Keller, R.N.
James Keller, M.D., Medical
    and Program Director,
    Chemical Dependency and
    Co-Dependency Programs,
    Halterman Center

After the work we have both done with Sharon, we feel a new freedom to be open and honest with each other about our wants and needs and, for the first time in 25 years of marriage, we feel like separate persons who can choose to be intimate.

Mary Seymour
Gary Seymour

Two long-term and entrenched co-dependents living together makes for a complicated relationship. Since our working day is spent together, our lives are perhaps more intricately intertwined than most. Although we had each done much individual work on ourselves, Sharon's workshop helped us to take a fresh look at our marriage from the viewpoint of a couple, rather than individuals who happened to be married to each other. Our mutual co-dependence couldn't resist the community of love and the laughter and tears we shared.

Thomas W. Perrin and
Janice Treggett
Managing Directors
Perrin & Treggett, Booksellers

_____CONTENTS_____

_____FOREWORD_____

Although there's a natural human tendency to form pair-bonds, this bonding process often seems to be haphazard, with no guarantee that a mutually satisfying coupleship will form. As George B. Leonard once pointed out, "We can orbit the earth, touch the moon . . . And yet this society has not devised a way (though love propels our very existence) for man and woman to live together for seven straight days with any assurance of harmony."

This book is about coupleship — learning to live together for seven straight days (and more) with the assurance of harmony. I consider coupleship to be the passionate spiritual, emotional and sexual commitment which nurtures _both_ partners in a relationship — a commitment which maintains a high regard for the value of each partner.

Sometimes it seems as if harmonious relationships are rare and exceptional in a world where the cruel and dispiriting rule of disharmony reigns supreme. No matter where I travel in my work, I hear the same comments:

- "I'm having trouble in my relationship."
- "Things aren't working out the way I expected."
- "We don't seem to talk, we don't seem to have anything in common. I wonder if we ever did . . ."
- "Close? I wouldn't say we're close. Even when we make love, it's like we're in different worlds."

- "I don't think we even like each other any more. We just live alone together."

I've heard and overheard so many similar comments, so many similar confessions of shattered dreams and so many admissions of abandoned hopes that I decided to interview a few couples who were really satisfied and happy in their relationships. I found people eager to talk about their relationships, but only a few couples seemed to have found their way to a relatively happy and satisfying coupleship. There were many more who quietly and painfully shared their hurts, fears and disappointments.

Like all relationships, couples come in many varieties and form a continuum from loose short-term affiliation to deep long-term commitment and union. For example, in a study of 400 successful men and their wives married 15-25 years, J.F. Cuber and Peggy B. Harroff found four groups stood out: Vital (about 1/6th of the couples), Congenial (1/3), Devitalized (about 1/3) and Combative (1/6).

The **Vital Couples** viewed themselves as having an active affectional and sexual life and enjoyed many interests and activities in common. Their marriages were rewarding and genuinely happy.

The **Congenial Couples** also rated themselves as being happily married, but lacked the vitality and energetic involvement of the vital group. They demanded little of each other and met most of their personal needs by occupying themselves with children, friends or work.

The **Devitalized Couples** expressed nostalgia — and frequently bitterness — about the vanished vitality in their marriages. They outwardly enjoyed the reputation of having a successful marriage, but their devitalized marriage left them resentful and empty. Practical reasons kept them together — children, a prosperous lifestyle, the importance of maintaining a front for friends and relatives and the lack of attractive alternatives.

The **Combative Couples** were the unhappiest of all and were enmeshed in continual conflict and power struggles. They rarely displayed affection or support for each other and when they did, it was for show, an empty gesture for public consumption.

Not all couples, of course, fall into neat and tidy categories. The life cycle of a couple passes through many changes, and the couple alliance brings up many complex issues.

In this book, I have concentrated mainly on two groups of couples. Both groups are made up of heterosexual couples — some married, some not.

1. **The Spirited or Centered Couple** express satisfaction about the relationship. The partners feel happy and fulfilled. Their coupleship not only works, it thrives.

2. **The Spiritually Dead or Estranged Couple** express dissatisfaction about the relationship. The partners feel lonely, hurt and angry. Their coupleship remains unfulfilled.

In addition to the many people I've interviewed, I have also drawn upon my experiences with thousands of couples I have worked with in the last 17 years. Some of those couples were enrolled in college. Others lived in suburban neighborhoods. Some were in the early years of partnering. Others had been together over 25 years. I have talked with the very wealthy and the very poor. I have counseled with military couples, rural couples, the ultra-sophisticated and with regular folk.

A major finding remains constant and clear regardless of the type of couple I've come into contact with: Some couples grow in togetherness with each other, and year after year become closer and more loving. Other couples grow apart, becoming more and more distant to each other with each passing year. I intend to explore both kinds of interactions in this book.

More specifically, I hope my discussion of the achievement and maintenance of coupleship will be useful in pointing the direction to practical answers to the important questions concerning your own relationship:

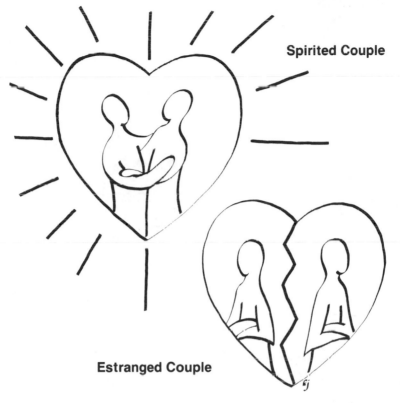

Spirited Couple

Estranged Couple

- What is intimacy and do you want it? And how do you recognize it when you have it?
- What is coupleship and how do you create it in your relationship?
- What breaks up partners?
- Do you want a commitment? How do you know when you've made a commitment?
- What can you do as a partner to be happier in your relationship?
- What can be done to create or renew coupleship?

Above all, I wish for you and your partner the vision to make wise choices as you examine and find new ways of enhancing your coupleship.

Sharon Wegscheider-Cruse
Onsite
2820 West Main
Rapid City, South Dakota 57702

PART 1

Explorations in Coupleships

1

Intimacy

*To cheat oneself out of love is the most terrible
deception, it is an eternal loss for which there is
no reparation, either in time or in eternity.*
— *Kierkegaard*

You can only give away what you have. That is the miracle
of intimacy and that is the hope of every close relationship.
If you have love and the ability to be intimate, you can give
it away. If you don't have love or the ability to be intimate,
you have nothing to give. But it's not only a matter of giving.
Love and intimacy always involve reciprocation — openness
and emotional sharing between partners.

Sad to say, then, that there can be much togetherness in
human relationships, yet so very little sharing, so very little
true intimacy. I've often seen a clinging kind of togetherness, where one partner seems to want to merge their own
personality into the other partner. I've also seen the kind of
togetherness where a couple lives under the same roof, but

remains aloof and apart almost like distant relatives or tenants in an apartment house.

"We are all so much together," said Albert Schweitzer, "but we are all dying of loneliness."

Intimacy is a basic human need, and it shouldn't be confused with the need for sex. Sex can be an important aspect of intimacy, but sex is not the only — or even the most important — kind of sharing. We will do much exploring of our sexual selves further in this book. However, in this chapter I want to focus on our emotional selves.

Before we can find and *maintain* sexual satisfaction with a partner, we must develop our ability to achieve and *maintain* "emotional intercourse". What do I mean by emotional intercourse? It grows from the desire to connect with someone else — to learn what that person thinks and feels, and to share, in return, your innermost self.

Emotional Connecting

There are many ways of connecting emotionally with your partner. You can reach intimacy through exchanging stories, expressing feelings, listening, doing things together, being emotionally vulnerable with each other and showing physical affection to each other.

Here are a couple of examples of connecting emotionally during times of stress:

David and Karen

When David announced to Karen that he was going out of the country for a three-week business trip, Karen immediately felt rejected, discounted and angry. When Karen expressed these feelings, David felt unappreciated and misunderstood.

The tension and painful feelings could have remained deadlocked. Sarcasm and the "silent treatment" were an old pattern for David and Karen. Fortunately, once they realized just how stuck, hurt and deadlocked they were, they decided to open up — to become much more vulnerable with each other.

David explained that he felt a growing inadequacy with his peers. He was worried and felt under a lot of pressure because there were so many new, younger and seemingly brighter co-workers in his department. The competition was subdued, but fierce. To David the trip out of the country was a reassurance of his worth to his company.

"I really need this chance to show what I can do," David confided.

When David talked about his fears, inadequacy and hope for affirmation, Karen began to listen — almost for the first time — and she began to understand. This gave her a new perspective, and for once she did not feel rejected and excluded from the decision.

Karen, in turn, told David about her feelings of being left behind, which fed into her fears of abandonment and non-importance.

"Whenever something like this comes up, I just feel so lonely and isolated," she told David, without a blaming and accusing tone in her voice.

As he listened, David began to understand Karen's fear and hurt. And he began to think more about ways of staying in touch and including Karen in all of his travel plans. By actions and words, he assured Karen that she was important to him. Because of their sharing, Karen and David became closer than ever.

Tom and Kay

Tempers were short and feelings high Christmas morning at the Blockmeiers. Tom and Kay had invited their parents for Christmas and nothing seemed to be going right. There had been transportation delays, heavy traffic and very little rest for anyone the night before. Today everyone was cranky. And on top of everything else, the furnace had broken down.

Tom felt tense as his dad peered over his shoulder and gave him advice on how to fix the belt on the furnace. "How long has it been since you had this furnace serviced?" Tom's dad asked, without waiting for answer. "That belt's way overdue for a change and there's sure a lot of dust and grime on the motor. These furnaces need a lot of upkeep — if you'd taken better care of it, the furnace wouldn't have broken down this morning, that's for sure." Tom grunted and bit his tongue. It *was* Christmas after all.

Kay was fixing coffee and hot chocolate and trying to keep everyone happy and cheerful and comfortable on a cold morning. Her mother kept reminding Kay that furnaces, appliances and other labor-saving devices needed attention and care. "This whole situation could have been so easily avoided," Kay's mother sighed, casting a critical glance around the kitchen as if to see what else was being neglected by Tom and Kay.

By the time the house was beginning to warm up, everyone was short with each other. Kay fixed two cups of coffee and invited Tom to the bedroom. Tom's first response was, "Now what?" Kay sat down and met Tom eye to eye and said, "Let's talk."

Each shared their reprimands by their respective parents. Tom and Kay talked about their anger at being criticized unfairly. They both felt disappointment and hurt because their parents didn't seem to be able to show any appreciation — just grumpiness and criticism.

They were able to support and comfort each other, and after 30 minutes or so of closeness and sharing their feelings, they both felt recharged. A bit of healing had taken place through a much-needed session of intimacy. They were ready to share in the holiday spirit.

> *You deserve lots of hugs and kisses.*
> *But do you have the tools to learn how to be*
> *huggable and kissable?*

Passion

The passionate attraction and energy between two lovers can generate a profound ecstasy and sense of well-being. Where does passion come from? A clue lies in one definition of the word "passion": To be passionate is to be "full of life". If we are passionate, we will necessarily experience ourselves as being "full of life".

Although passion can be the source of intense happiness between couples, it can also generate in times of pain and stress, the most penetrating suffering. I am fully convinced that love and passion are not fantasies or idealistic impossible dreams. Love and passion are great possibilities open to people who want to work for them. *Achieving* and *maintaining* an intimate and passionate relationship is both an adventure and a challenge.

It's important to keep in mind that the intimate and passionate relationship depends on these two things: Achieving the relationship and maintaining it. Both are essential to the development of coupleship. And both involve quite different skills. Many times people focus on the *achievement* of intimacy and neglect *maintenance,* as if once achieved, intimacy will run on automatic pilot without further attention.

Nothing could be further from the truth. Unless special attention is given to the maintenance of intimacy, passion wanes, indifference sets in and the honeymoon is over in more ways than one. Continued neglect of the relationship inevitably turns it from a passionate coupleship into a kind of bland pairing where only impersonal things are shared.

The Roots of Intimacy

If we want to achieve intimacy, where do we begin? Many psychologists have written about the "child within", and many therapy models are based on getting in touch with the inner child. Simply put, the child within is that part of ourself that is innocent, lovable, emotionally responsive and wonderfully vulnerable as it puts forth its effort to grow. Many people have been able to recapture some tender and compassionate parts of themselves by remembering and caring for their inner child.

The exploration of your inner child can be a helpful aid in relating to your partner — you become more aware of your partner's own inner child. To be interested in and caring for the child within your partner is a major step toward intimacy. Each partner can explore the power of vulnerability, the power and energy that is released by letting others know who you are, without defenses or excuses.

But the achievement and maintenance of intimacy go much further than getting in touch with your inner child. There are hundreds of good books about "love" and people continue to go to movies to see love stories. And thousands of songs have been written about love. Yet too few people see love as a *choice* and a *commitment* of time, money and energy. In order to thrive, love requires much care and attention.

For most people, the problem of love is simple and self-focused: "I don't feel loved enough." However, I believe that behind this feeling of love-deprivation there's a much more complex process going on. Feeling unloved is probably valid — as far as it goes. But it's only the tip of the iceberg. Most often the problem of love is not that we are unloved by others, but that we have not developed our own capacity to love.

> *It is not that we have not been loved enough, it is that we have not learned "to love".*
>
> — *Sam H.*

Love Skills

Learning to love is a skill. (Please note I'm not talking about sexual skills and techniques — which may be important aspects of relationships, but are not the be-all and end-all of loving relationships.) Learning to love doesn't "just happen" if we meet the right person. Feeling love may come naturally, but to be effective in an intimate relationship, loving feelings must go hand in hand with loving behavior. And for most of us, loving behavior must be learned. The implication: If we want to learn to love, we must proceed as if we want to learn a skill, such as nursing, accounting, carpentry, typing and so on.

There are two parts to learning a skill. First, we can learn the theory or the lessons involved and be able to identify the ingredients of love and loving. The second part entails practice, for like any other skill, practice makes perfect. The tennis player doesn't develop a solid serve simply by watching the masters play or by reading a book on "Basics of The Championship Serve". The reliable, accurate serve doesn't come as a result of feeling like a terrific tennis player and loving the game intensely. It comes from practice, from training, from feedback and from trial and error.

Similarly, the lessons of love must be practiced, must be put to work. With concentration. With dedication. And that's the hard part. Over and over I have worked with people who say they hunger for closer ties. They say they want more intimacy and better relationships. But while they insist they crave closeness, they will put almost everything ahead of their commitment to love. I have seen success, prestige, sports, TV, money, children — and virtually anything else — take priority over the commitment, time and energy necessary for cultivating intimacy.

As we begin any new skill in our life, we feel awkward and bumbling, and each effort feels new and strange. Just as our bodies feel different after just one week of walking or exercise, so do our emotions; and our feelings of closeness take on new dimensions after one week of new awareness. As a matter of fact, it gets exciting to realize that paying attention to a coupleship can be both stimulating and exciting.

Most people see marriage or coupleship as a fusion of two people. Another way of looking at this intimate relationship is seeing it as a partnership interested in the welfare of each partner. We all have curiosity about the purpose of life (if our curiosity has not been stifled). Perhaps one purpose of coupleship is to help each other make the quest — to understand and develop the self, and to seek and find meaning in life.

It's a great help and comfort when one is sitting on a pile of horse manure to have someone who is watching tell you, "That's horse manure — not red roses". Clear direct feedback from someone who cares is a gift we get as we develop a coupleship. In the acceptance of our many denials and delusions, we find the solution to our loneliness and isolation.

Positive Intention

Once each person in a coupleship declares that they "want it to be better", they can develop an attitude I call "positive intention". Positive intention and actual behavior are two different things. Yet if partners are willing to talk and share, many conflicts can be avoided or easily resolved. There are some basic guidelines a couple agrees to as they begin to move deeper into a coupleship:

1. **Honesty of Feelings** — Feelings of passion and feelings of vulnerability are both needed. Couples give each other permission to voice anger, disappointment and jealousy. In addition, each partner is willing to share hurt, guilt, inadequacy and fear.
2. **Courage** — Each person contributes to the partnership even if it is scary or threatening. They expect no more from the partnership than they are ready to give.
3. **Spontaneity** — Even though each partner respects and values each other's responsibilities and time commitments, each is willing to put a bookmark in self-activity to respond to the *want* or *need* of the other.
4. **Responsibility** — As we become more aware of the impact we have on those around us, we are able to respond in loving ways. Learning to say, "I don't understand", "I am sorry", "Will you tell me again", or "It was my fault" — all of these admissions and

responses get easier and easier. We learn that the goal is closeness, support and intimacy rather than winning, power and control.

5. **Diversity** — We learn about the richness of differences. When we *really* get to know another person wholly, we discover ideas, thoughts and values that are a bit different (or a lot different) from our own. We then have new possibilities for learning and can *invite* differentness instead of fearing and rejecting it. We can appreciate human diversity instead of having to defeat it or feeling inadequate.

It gets easier and easier to think in terms of a coupleship. As we do so, we almost automatically come to consider our partner's feelings, thoughts and welfare.

Before we are ready to shower love on another person, or before we are ready to love anyone specific, we need to develop the ability to love in general. Love is more than just a relationship to a person. Love is an attitude, a skill and a part of one's character or personhood. Love can be seen in the way we relate to the world. Love has very little to do with the object of our love.

Aspects of Love

As we practice different kinds of love, we prepare ourselves for a specific love and commitment to one person. The practicing of love includes the love toward a good friend (an intimate connection), parenting love (bonding), self-love (knowing and appreciating ourselves) and spiritual love (discovering meaning in our lives). Let's take a closer look at each of these aspects of love:

- **Friends and Relatives** — This is a general love between equals. It includes the care, support, respect and interest we give another. We overlook our faults, respect our differences, and relish each other's company. We come together because at a very human level we have much in common. We have chosen to be there for each other in the ups and downs of life.

> *We are more alike than we are different*
> *and we all need to be loved.*

- **Parenting Love** — The love of a parent toward a child is a special kind of bonding. Through good times and bad times, there is an intensity of connection. There is a sense of connectedness that takes on the care and responsibility for the child's life and growth. The parent's ability to give to the child will be determined by the parent's ability to know what that child's needs are. However, the desire to give and protect that child are present in that parent's love.

> *To love others fully, you must have been*
> *loved yourself. Parents often cannot give*
> *what they themselves never received.*

- **Self-love** — It's time to put to rest the fallacy that it's selfish to love oneself. Love is an attitude which is the same toward self and others: It's an ability to care for another. The Bible speaks of self-love when it commands you to "love thy neighbor as thyself". That command implies that we respect our own integrity and uniqueness. In loving yourself, you will discover all of yourself. The development of this uniqueness and the full knowledge of yourself is what you have to offer a partnership.

> *The love and knowledge you have of yourself*
> *is what you have to offer a partner.*

• **Spiritual Love** — The acceptance of a Higher Power or God springs from the need to overcome the sense of isolation and to achieve order and union. Love, connectedness, trust, belonging — are all elements of our spiritual selves. The sharing of a spiritual self with a partner is a self-transcending form of intimacy.

Sharing our spiritual selves is essential to the growth of intimacy in coupleship.

Intimacy, like love, does not come naturally. It is not easy to attain. It is not all hearts and roses. Intimacy requires confrontation and conflict. It requires expressing feelings, sharing our innermost selves and sometimes fighting it out. If you leave significant issues unresolved for any length of time, anger and hurt fester and distance widens. In many instances, intimacy weakens or dies.

Essential Ingredients of Intimacy

I've put together a set of guidelines to becoming an intimate partner — a few hints and clues to help you begin to recognize some of the essential ingredients of intimacy:

... You do not need to be totally self-sacrificing or self-effacing. You do not need to surrender your life to another. You can give generously, freely and joyfully. You can also choose to give to yourself, generously, freely and joyfully.

... You know you are okay and self-satisfied with your own esteem and goodness. From a position of self-esteem, you can recognize that you are enhanced by the partner you love because the partner brings our your "okayness" and gives it a special luster.

. . . You are able to openly tell your partner how important he/she is to you and invite your partner to share more aspects of your life.

. . . You will be able to plan for a future together and make a firm commitment to each other. You will be able to stay committed and alive with a sense of humor through the setbacks and the problems and the inevitable hard times.

. . . You will be able to accept your partner's shortcomings and faults and not demand change.

. . . After the rush of early passion, you will want to be committed to growing and changing and keeping the passion alive.

In a passionate relationship you will be able to get up each day, look at your partner and say, "Today, I voluntarily and freely commit myself to this relationship". If it's true, celebrate! If the words catch in your throat (as they sometimes may), talk it out immediately. If your relationship is alive and well, your partner will respond in such a way that the words will again be easy to say. On the other hand, if you get a negative or indifferent response from your partner, the relationship obviously needs extra attention.

Attention to the relationship lies at the core of every caring coupleship — attention to the relationship, to your partner and to your own needs. When attention wanes, neglect, complacency, and indifference set in. Couples become devitalized and estranged. They become polite (or not so polite) associates, bound by proximity and routine. Just as flowers wither and die from inadequate care, so do vital relationships change into dry and brittle arrangements.

Touch

Touch is an important barometer of the aliveness of a relationship. We yearn to be touched. The nerves directly under the skin are stimulated by touch and carry signals to the brain. In turn, the brain transmits signals throughout the body — signals that cause muscles to relax and the heart rate and blood pressure to fall.

Skin is the largest organ of the body and, as Ashley Montagu stresses in *Touching*, "Perhaps next to the brain, the skin is the most important of all our organ systems." Until recently what Montagu calls the "human significance" of the skin has been overlooked in the study of relationships. Skin has many jobs:

- Skin is a sensitive receiver of information . . .
- Skin communicates (blushing, livid with rage, ashen with fear) . . .
- Skin protects us from harmful elements in the environment.

There have been many studies over the years that provide evidence of significant biochemical differences between humans who have enjoyed tactile stimulation (skin connection) and those who have not. These studies suggest that the "unloved" person is likely to be a very different biochemical entity from those who have been adequately loved, touched and stimulated in infancy.

The importance of touch has been repeatedly confirmed in experiments with animals, and without touch in infancy, humans fail to thrive. Touch deprivation stunts growth and may even prevent the later development of intimacy in adulthood. Without the soothing effect of touch, we experience increased anxiety, even a sense of loss.

We live in an age when people seem to feel more comfortable in reaching out to extra-terrestrial beings than in reaching out to a friend. The sophistication of current technology often leaves us "skin hungry". Skin hunger is simply the desire to be touched and affirmed physically. We frequently seek to connect with words.

We . . .

— Brainstorm
— Intellectualize
— Discuss the ways of the world
— Shoot the breeze

. . . and so on — when we are simply hungry for physical touch.

The true language of sex between two people is primarily non-verbal. Words are inadequate when compared with the feelings sensed and the contacts that physically take place between us. The words "I love you" can run the risk of becoming merely routine, but a gentle touch of support at critical times is worth a thousand words. The power of physical sexual contact is explosive and can sometimes be life-changing.

The need for body contact exists. Many substitutes are tried — food, tobacco, alcohol, drugs, work, success, power and exercise — all can be used to try to satisfy skin hunger and the need for body contact. Sex can also be a substitute, for the only way some people can get the body contact they need when they merely want to be touched or held and comforted, is by giving or asking for sex. Thus many sexual encounters are attempts to satisfy skin hunger, hunger for affection.

These contacts are usually brief and ultimately dissatisfying. Instead of a warm afterglow, depression sets in. The truly lucky are those whose coupleship can satisfy the skin hunger of each other and through commitment and love remain invested after contact.

A person's need for body contact is essential. If that need is not satisfied, even though all other needs are satisfied, people will feel lonely and hurt. It's important that we begin to understand how necessary it is for us to touch, be close and offer affection.

Lack of touch is experienced as separation anxiety. It can only be relieved by contact and connection. The loss of human physical contact brings about feelings of loneliness, frustration and a lack of emotional warmth.

Touch and the affirmation it brings is an essential part of coupleship. Sexual touching and coupling are important aspects of contact, but there are many other ways of non-sexual touching that increase bonding between those who love.

Casual touching is very easy for some people and extremely difficult for others. Finding your own and your partner's pleasure points enhances the couple alliance and is always a part of developing coupleship. Check it out with your partner!

1. Some physical touch in public — a touch to shoulder, arm, hand and so on.
2. Some intimate hand-holding and touching in public places.
3. Arm around the other . . . in a car, in a theater, at the table at a dinner party, at home while visiting with others, while watching TV.
4. Touching each other on knee or other part of the body while . . . in a theater, driving a car, visiting with others, watching TV.
5. Discuss preferences, experiment, respect — and above all . . . Enjoy!

Again, touch is essential to coupleship and helps create and maintain the strong sense of intimacy which comforts and strengthens both partners and helps them cope with the stresses of everyday life. Through intimate contact — through touch — we gain the power to face the world knowing we can always retreat to a haven of renewal.

Myths About Intimacy

We must discard several myths before we begin to work on the partnership:

1. Having an affair can help a faltering marriage.
2. It's important to keep a marriage together for the sake of the children.
3. When two people rarely argue or fight, that's a sign of a happy marriage.
4. It's possible to expect another person to fulfill your needs.
5. After two people have been together for a while, it's common to lose sexual interest in each other.

6. If you only had enough money, the marriage would never have any problems.
7. You'll get to know each other better with time.
8. If sex is good, intimacy will follow.

Sexual intimacy can be a very important ingredient in a relationship, but sex is not the ultimate expression of intimacy. On the contrary, emotional intercourse, not sexual intercourse, paves the way to intimacy. Emotional intercourse is a way of life. As partners engage in this kind of emotional closeness, there may be very intense and satisfying sexual intercourse from time to time. However, the more frequent satisfying intercourse will be emotional intercourse.

Most of us are touch-starved. We haven't had appropriate experience with touch. We haven't learned how to touch and be touched. In a real sense, we are out of touch with touch.

Touch deprivation plays a key role in the development of marital and sexual problems. One of the things you can do is to stop worrying about having intercourse and achieving orgasm and just enjoy each other's touch. Once sexual intercourse becomes just one of the possibilities in a relationship, rather than its primary focus and goal, you and your partner are free to be more creative and more responsive to each other's needs.

Some people can remember back to times when, for whatever reason, it was not possible to share sexual intercourse. They became adept at arousing each other and often experienced fulfilling orgasms without intercourse. They could share sensuality because of a deeper involvement — because their depth of emotional intercourse enabled them to enjoy each other sensually without sex.

Prime Time

An important concept in achieving sexual intimacy is *prime time*. Prime time means the best time. Instead of squeezing sexual time into late evening or early morning or on vacation, the couple plans prime time into their lifestyle.

This does not mean a rigid structuring of sexual time together, with a grim determination to have mutual orgasms on every sexual contact or arousal. Such orgasms, induced repeatedly in the same mechanical way, sputter to completion, rather than explode as the result of ever-increasing levels of ecstasy.

Prime time means planning time together to relax and share. While sex is not the purpose of prime time, it may be the result. It's important to set aside time for dinner, to go walking, to hold hands, to see a movie, to go dancing or to swim. What is important is the use of prime time for two people only, to build an environment where intimacy can grow and oftentimes grow into a sexual encounter. In prime time the rule is: Two is company, three's a crowd.

Why is prime time so important? Intimate feelings are fragile and can't be expected to survive the floods and drought of day-to-day living without the shelter of planned time.

Privacy

The demands for sharing and giving are so intense in intimate relationships that either partner may need to retreat into the self at times to reaffirm individuality and re-energize. These natural breaks would be threatening to a person with low self-worth, but are clearly understood by a partner with high self-worth who experiences the same need.

In a satisfying relationship, these times of privacy and solitude are not viewed as signs of rejection or abandonment, but as necessary periods of personal recharging — an interlude before the next close and intimate time.

Peaks of intimacy are oftentimes more appreciated in contrast to periodic and appropriate distancing. When you come together again after a period of separation, your relationship is intensified.

Intimacy thrives in coupleship. And without intimacy a coupleship becomes devitalized, distant and estranged. Couples may exist without intimacy, but without intimacy they must forever remain acquaintances only.

> *Remember to let the winds of heaven*
> *dance between you.*
>
> *— Ralph Blum*

2

Coupleship

*"Coupleship" is a passionate spiritual —
emotional — sexual commitment between two
people that nurtures both people and maintains
a high regard for the value of each person.*

A relationship is a dynamic process between one person
and another person, place, substance or event. A relationship can be *to:*

- a person (parent, sibling, friend, lover, etc.)
- one's pet
- possessions, car, jewelry
- job, role

A relationship to something takes the form of a *one-sided
attachment* to a person, a pet, possessions, a job.

Contrast the one-sided attachment with a different kind of
relationship — a *dynamic relationship characterized by
mutual attachment.* A relationship with a lover, a friend, a

pet or an employer are all examples of a relationship *with* —
when there is a mutual attachment or reciprocation.

A coupleship, then, is a kind of an enhanced relationship,
a relationship-plus. Two people who *choose* a relationship
with each other can admit to building a "*coupleship*".

In thinking about coupleship, it might help to look at
what Anita and Robert Taylor call "the couple alliance". This
alliance consists of a contract — expressed and implied. The
alliance has a trajectory that covers depth and duration. And
the couple alliance has continuity. The Taylors go on to say:

> "Couple unions may be of long or brief
> duration, superficial or deep in intensity, man-
> dated or freely negotiated, supportive or destruc-
> tive, pleasurable or agonizing, familiar or bizarre.
> Whatever the nature of the relationship, the
> commitment of two people to form a couple
> initiates couple dynamics that are independent of
> the individuals. The couple, based upon the
> goals, efforts and interactions of the two people
> involved has a life of its own and encounters
> changes, both predictable and unexpected."

Inertia can play a role in the continuity of a couple.
According to Newtonian physics, a body in motion tends to
remain in motion. Similarly the Taylors note that a couple,
through inertia, tends to persist and survive major crises. "By
the same theory, a body at rest tends to remain at rest and
many couple unions continue in a state of ennui or
disinterested coexistence, persisting for no better reason
than that no stress has been sufficient to bring the final
split."

Before getting too deep into the dynamics of the couple,
it might help at this point to look at coupleship readiness.

Coupleship Readiness

We are ready for this kind of committed relationship when we have developed independence in important areas of our lives: socially, emotionally, financially, mentally and physically.

When one is **emotionally independent**, one takes responsibility for one's feelings. Take Janet and Ron, for example. For the most part, they enjoy their relationship, yet there are certain times when Ron becomes sullen, distant and sarcastic. This causes Janet to feel helpless, lonely and angry. This kind of interaction happened repeatedly during the first years of their marriage. Finally, Janet insisted they seek outside help. After just five sessions with a marriage counselor, both Janet and Ron found a pattern. In Ron's childhood, his mother had been needy and demanding following the death of Ron's father.

Now whenever we have a bit of "unfinished business" with a parent, it shows up in current relationships. Ron found that as Janet talked with him about home, job and responsibilities, he heard his "mother's" voice and rebelled as he had as a child and teenager. Ron recognized the pattern as it unfolded in counseling, and he realized that he was blaming and projecting his emotional hangover on to Janet.

Ron then took responsibility for his own emotions. He joined a men's group and learned more about his feelings and behavior. He took responsibility and became *emotionally independent*. The quality of sharing between him and Janet increased.

Social independence is also important to a coupleship. It means developing the capacity to make and maintain friendships that enhance a couple's union. (I want to make a clear distinction between these kinds of friendships and other personal friendships that split couples, cause jealousy and drain energy. What I mean by social independence is taking the responsibility to create friendships that enhance the coupleship.)

Bill and Caroline worked out their conflicts around over-dependence some years ago. Bill is a skier — it's been his favorite sport since he was a little boy. Caroline, on the other hand, is an indoor person who likes to read and do needlepoint. Bill used to resent Caroline's resistance to their ski trips, and felt deprived if they didn't go. Caroline felt controlled if she went on a ski jaunt just to please Bill. After a long talk about their needs and wants, Bill made a decision to find a ski buddy.

Bill took the initiative to check around and discovered a co-worker, Frank, who was in virtually the same situation. The issue of social independence was resolved simply: Twice a year Bill and Frank plan skiing vacations. At the conclusion of each trip, Caroline and Frank's mate join Bill and Frank for a couple of days of sightseeing. Both Caroline and Bill fulfill their own social needs and coupleship needs without having to depend totally on each other for friendship and recreation.

By **mental independence** I mean that each person keeps stimulated and interested in a variety of subjects, and that the partners use their learning to enrich each other, thereby enriching the coupleship. When we attain mental independence, we think for ourselves, form our own opinions, seek our own information, make our own judgments. We have varied interests — like Ted and Jean.

Ted has a great interest in computers, sports, camping and hiking, medicine and music. He reads magazines, trade journals, attends conferences and keeps current in many subjects. Jean has an interest in current events, politics, local news, business and accounting. She, too, keeps well-informed and up-to-date. Jean and Ted look forward to their sharing time together. Each takes responsibility to provide the other with new information and stimulating ideas.

Physical independence includes taking care of one's own body care. This includes personal hygiene, diet, smoke-free breath and body cleanliness, appearance and so on. I have often been surprised to find how frequently one partner is turned off by a habit or physical condition of the other partner — and I have also been surprised to find how difficult it is to get couples to express their dissatisfaction with the mate.

By **financial independence** I mean each person's financial contribution to the relationship. There needs to be a monetary value placed on home services when couples decide that one partner will "work in the home". The antiquated idea that one provides finances and the other provides home life has proved to be a loss for everyone concerned. It's important that both partners take responsibility for home chores, social life, emotional environment and child care — and especially so when both couples work. And it's also a good idea for each partner to have a sense of financial contribution and freedom. A certain measure of financial independence can be attained when each partner has a personal checking (or savings) account and there's a joint account for family and joint business ventures.

Thus we prepare for coupling by becoming a whole independent person. Then the whole person is ready to meet with another whole person and work toward the caring commitment called "coupleship".

Too often, a fragmented, incomplete person looks to a partner to fill the void in self. When there are parts of our self that are not developed, we have a strong inclination to look for a partner to fill our own void. If we feel deficient in certain areas of our lives, we may be drawn to someone we see as stronger, more competent — someone, in short, who does not have our own deficiencies.

Sometimes a very shy person will be attracted to an aggressive person or an outgoing person. In the early stages of the partnership, the shy person is relieved of much responsibility as the more aggressive person takes on the responsibility. This will work for a period of time. However, if the shy person wants to become more assertive, there may be stress as the traditional roles change and conventional expectations are challenged.

Shy is attracted to outgoing — later feels controlled.
Outgoing is attracted to shy — later feels bored.

Strong is attracted to fragile — later resents feeling responsible.

Fragile is attracted to strong — later feels controlled and discounted.

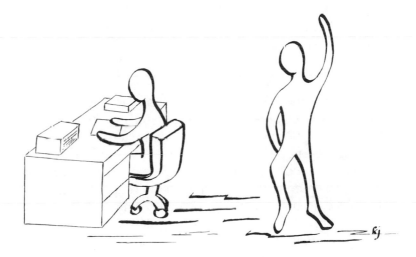

Charm and fun is attracted to serious — later is bored and feels stifled.

Serious is attracted to charm and fun — later resents people intruding on privacy.

Generous is attracted to conservative — later feels controlled.

Conservative is attracted to generous — later resents too much giving away and feels used.

> *"Coupleship" is the enhanced relationship between two whole healthy and happy individuals.*

There are other possibilities. For example, the time may come when the more aggressive person gets tired of the responsibility. When two people become attracted to each other out of need, both must remain in need for the relationship to continue. If one or both partners find ways to fill their own needs, then a change in the original partnering takes place. Couples may then begin to "uncouple".

Partners in the process of uncoupling have a strained relationship that may survive in some form for a long time, but the odds are against coupleship under such circumstances.

The Humanizing Process

Psychiatrist Robert Seidenberg maintains that marriage can provide the couples a means to hasten what he calls the "humanizing" process — "opportunities for accommodation, for individuation, for the exchange of ideals and values, for the delineation of boundaries, for the testing of moralities and the mastery of erring instincts."

Seidenberg goes on to say: "All of these are apt to be purely theoretical until one is confronted with the realities of the everyday give and take which the intimacy of marriage provides. Here, then, can be an opportunity for getting to know what and who one really is, instead of retaining theoretical images that one has lived up until then. One can then find out how generous, how tolerant, how unselfish, how brilliant one really is."

Ideals thus undergo a painful testing — testing in the real world, not a fantasy world, not a dream world. "In marriage lies the opportunity of eliminating self-myths . . ." Seidenberg views marriage as a great leveler, a "a societal head-

1 Partner
+ 1 Partner
_____
1 Coupleship

shrinker which, for some, ends illusions about self-importance, courage, honesty, integrity and generosity. And they are better for it."

Marriage may prove to those who have low self-esteem that they possess great resources — "greater moral fiber than they have ever dreamt."

Seidenberg concludes: ". . . all is theoretical and abstract until put to the test of intimacy which only marriage is likely to provide. *Genuine growth comes only with satisfaction and frustrations, in which learning and doing are inextricably involved.*"

That is the growth which occurs in coupleship.

Perhaps one of the most important concepts to understand about coupleship is that it enhances the individual lives of each of the partners. Coupleship always exists between two people who have a commitment, not only to each other, but to their relationship as well. They don't take it for granted — they appreciate it and often express a sense of joy and wonder that their coupleship has come into existence. They are committed to learning more about the relationship. They pay attention to it, care for it and protect it. And they revel in their coupleship and celebrate it.

The Synergy of Coupleship

Synergy occurs when two organisms or people are brought together or combined in such a way that the end result is enhanced — that is, when the combination of the two produces a quality or effect that is more intense than what either of the two contributing parts originally had or could independently attain. Thus, in synergy one and one makes three, not just two.
— *Neena O'Neill and George O'Neill*

In love, your union adds up to three: The synergy of your coupleship adds something extra to your lives and together you create a relationship that is greater than the sum of its parts. You maintain your uniqueness as individuals, but allow an easy, natural interdependence. Neena and George O'Neill call this process "synergic enhancement" or "couple power through person power".

In their book *Open Marriage* the O'Neills describe this synergy: "Like a chain reaction, synergy once begun builds upon itself, intensifying and expanding, and as it expands it feeds back new meanings, new discoveries, new explorations of self and mate into a self-reinforcing regenerative and growth-enhancing system that has no limits except those that you yourself set upon it."

Basic Coupleship Attitudes

In coupleship there are some basic attitudes that enhance trust, promote care and ultimately increase the feeling of safety and comfort. These following attitudes create a sense of well-being in both partners of a coupleship:

1. **Respect:** Respect means considering the thoughts and feelings of the other. It means learning what might hurt and avoiding those kinds of behaviors and comments. Kay shows respect when she asks Ken if he needs some quiet time at home before dinner. Ken shows respect when he calls Kay if he's going to be late. Respect means treating your partner with as much courtesy as you would treat a distinguished stranger.

2. **Encouragement:** Kay shows Ken encouragement when she supports his efforts to resolve a conflict with his family. She asks questions, shares her thoughts and feelings and asks for his. Ken shows encouragement as Kay tries to diet. He brings home a treat of fresh fish and suggests they walk together after dinner. There are no more gifts of candy, and dinners out are held to a minimum.

3. **Affirmation:** Both Glen and Nan have learned enough about each other to know each other's best points and to also know what each needs from the other. They

have developed a habit of noticing the best about each other and commenting on it.

Glen tells Nan she . . .

looks good in red . . . makes a great taco . . . has beautiful eyes . . . is exciting to be with . . .

Nan tells Glen he . . .

looks good in jeans . . . dances great . . . makes a superb salad . . . has a great sense of humor.

4. **Ability to Apologize:** Everyone makes mistakes. To be able to say, "I'm sorry" is a great enhancer of relationships. There is so much positive energy that can come from closeness that trying to prove who is right or who is wrong in a conflict is a major waste of precious time. When one is wrong, there is no need to rub it in or to spend a lot of time justifying it. It's much more important to say, "I'm sorry" and get on with life.

5. **Learning and Practicing a Feeling Vocabulary:** Often with someone we know well, we shortcut communication, expecting the other to intuitively sense our true meaning. Unfortunately, this doesn't always work, and misunderstandings arise. Intimacy means we try to be specific with our exact feelings — which isn't easy, because our feelings get mixed up. Nevertheless, it's worth the effort to learn to use feeling words, such as . . .

afraid	putdown	inadequate
humiliated	hurt	lonely
left out	vulnerable	controlled
helpless	grieved	off-balance
discounted	violated	insecure
abandoned	wrong	guilty

It is important to nurture ourselves and each other, and a key part of that nourishment comes from the basic attitudes of coupleship.

Coupleship and the intimacy that comes with it are the result of decisions we make about the kind of a relationship we want with a partner — and our determination to follow through and do what it takes to create coupleship.

> *Coupleship and the intimacy that comes with it depend on conscious decision and commitment.*

Boundaries

Reminders

*Never will I see a castle
And not think of you . . .
Wondering what might have been
Had we built the walls around us
Instead of between us.*
— *Royce Ellis Daniels*

In order to begin working on a coupleship and also to protect one, learning how to set boundaries is essential. Boundaries are the limits we set in order to protect our own well-being. Boundaries are a way that we teach those around us that we are important and our needs are important. It naturally follows that we respect other people's boundaries as well.

Boundaries are necessary in order to keep invaders from depleting the energy and marring the focus of the coupleship. It takes clarity and energy to make a relationship work, and the relationship must be protected from people, substances and events that drain energy and muddy the focus of our coupleship.

Many different kinds of stressors threaten the coupleship and I am going to discuss them in detail in the next section. For now, let's look at an illustration that may help clarify the concept of boundaries and invaders.

Boundaries simply indicate that someone or something is potentially so invasive to the coupleship that energy, which is needed to build a relationship, is drained away and the relationship suffers the loss. Couples establish boundaries to protect themselves from invasion and to conserve energy for the coupleship.

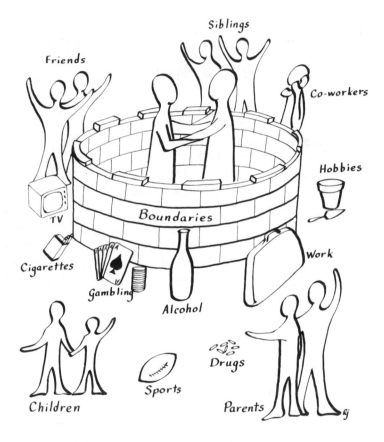

Coupleship: Mirage or Reality?

By now, you may be thinking that I am talking about the ideal or perfect relationship. *Coupleship sounds good on paper,* you think, *but it just sounds too good to be true.* You may think that coupleship is an elaborate fantasy or that if it does exist, it is exceedingly rare and terribly difficult to maintain.

Not so. In later chapters I will present several case histories of relationships that have achieved the kind of intimacy we find in coupleship, and I will describe the tools they used to achieve and maintain it. I will also give some examples of couples who did not invest in their relationships and I'll show how those relationships ended.

For now, consider this: Studies of happy marriages show that *companionability* and *respect* — not "love" — are the key words couples use to describe happy marriages. This point is elaborated by Lederer and Jackson in *The Mirages of Marriage*:

> "The happy, workable, productive marriage does not require love as defined in this book, or even the practice of the Golden Rule . . . Normal people should not be frustrated or disappointed if they are not in a *constant* state of love. If they experience the joy of love (or imagine they do) for ten per cent of the time they were married, attempt to treat each other with as much courtesy as they do distinguished strangers and attempt to make the marriage a workable affair — one where there are some practical advantages and satisfactions for each — the chances are that the marriage will endure longer and with more strength than the so-called love matches."

Lederer and Jackson sketch out the elements of a satisfactory marriage:

1. Spouses respect each other: The greater the number of areas of respect, the more satisfactory the marriage.
2. They are tolerant of each other: They see themselves as fallible, vulnerable human beings and can therefore accept each other's shortcomings.

3. They make an effort to make the most of assets and to minimize liabilities. Communication and negotiation play important roles in this process of accommodation: "A relationship is a process involving constant change; and constant change requires the spouses to *keep working on their relationship until the day they die.*"

. . . or else they become a "Gruesome Twosome".

Good News About Coupleship

The good news is that today in my work, I see more couples committed to intimacy and fulfillment than ever before. With the growing of self-worth in recovery from chemical dependency and co-dependency, people today are demanding more satisfaction from their relationships and are willing to work for it, willing to work toward coupleship.

The result? There are multiple winners, and partners express more satisfaction and happiness in their relationship. In many instances when parents work on their relationship, they begin to become positive role models for their children. Instead of seeing estranged or devitalized role models, children now have parents who can demonstrate their own loving behavior, grounded in self-worth and aimed at achieving and maintaining coupleship.

Love and intimacy are contagious, and families where coupleship reigns will produce future generations of healthy relationships.

3

Invaders I

Invaders are outside people, events, substances or attitudes that come between two people who are committed to each other. Invaders inevitably undermine and impair relationships. By depleting energy from the relationship, invaders interfere with the couple's capacity for care and reduce the intensity of their passion. Let's take a quick look at some of the types of invaders.

1. **People Invaders:** Each outside relationship has the potential to support and nourish a coupleship or to become an invader. Potential *people invaders* or *supporters* include . . .

    . . . friends
    . . . parents and siblings
    . . . children
    . . . support systems

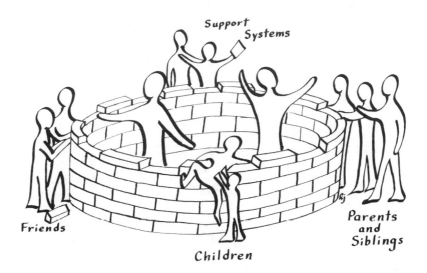

Support Systems

Friends

Children

Parents and Siblings

2. Substance Invaders: These invaders affect our health, judgment and attention. When we form compelling relationships with substance invaders, we neglect our relationships with people. *Substance invaders include . . .*
. . . alchohol
. . . drugs
. . . nicotine
. . . food

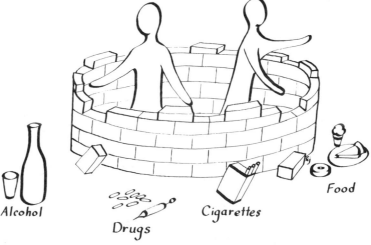

Alcohol

Drugs

Cigarettes

Food

3. **Behavioral Invaders:** These are habits that take time and energy away from our relationships. *Behavioral invaders* include . . .
   . . . gambling
   . . . sexual acting out
   . . . workaholism
   . . . television
   . . . sports

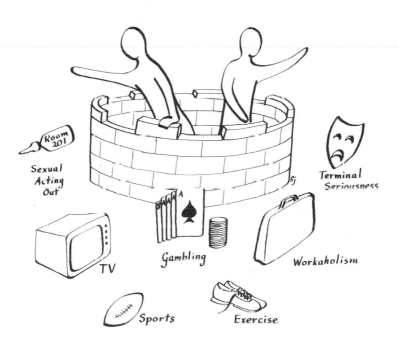

4. **Attitudinal Invaders:** These invaders involve thoughts, feelings and perceptions that color our outlook on life. *Attitudinal invaders* include . . .
   . . . myths
   . . . negativity
   . . . terminal seriousness

Now let's examine each of the invaders in more detail and see how they interfere with the development of coupleship.

People Invaders

Friends

Healthy relationships to friends nourish self-worth and are vital to our sense of well-being. Friends are people to share feelings with, to take trips with, to tell secrets to, to laugh with, to discuss ideas with. Friends offer support and encouragement and form a strong linkage in our support network.

When we have grown up in painful homes, we do not learn how to protect our boundaries. We give too much away in friendship. Friends become a drain, rather than a joy, because we are too open and too eager to please — at almost any cost.

Friends may also become over-dependent, demanding and emotionally exhausting. If we do not know how to set boundaries, we may try to emotionally purchase friends:

- We become caregivers — taking excess care of the needs of friends.
- We never disappoint friends even if we are inconvenienced.
- We respect friends' wants and wishes more than our own.
- We are willing and eager to take more than 50% of the responsibility for the friendship.
- We patiently listen to their problems, even if they choose not to get help.

Healthy friends will bring out the health in each of us. Only unhealthy relationships will impose on a coupleship in a negative way. Each person in the coupleship needs to discuss and understand the impact of healthy and unhealthy friendships on the coupleship. Healthy friendships will enhance the coupleship.

Parents and Siblings

Many people (not all) have come from homes where their emotional needs and physical needs were not met. This could happen for many reasons: One or both of the parents may have been involved in alcoholism or other chemical dependency, mental illness or workaholism. Home life may have been disrupted by frequent relocations, chronic sickness in a family member or early death of a parent, poverty, extreme religiosity, painful divorce . . . and on and on.

For any number of reasons a parent may have been under severe emotional strain, or the parents' relationship might have been full of antagonism, frustration and fear. When parents are upset, the children sense the pain, grow confused and then come to feel responsible for the turmoil in the family. Stressed-out parents have little time or attention to give the children. This leaves a child hungry for love and attention. The child learns to get love and attention by giving it — by becoming a caretaker.

While the parents remain in the authoritative position in regard to expectations and behavior, the child takes on responsibility for the emotional well-being of the parents. Dysfunctional families come in many styles and varieties, but they all share one similarity: The children who come from these families assume excessive responsibility for the well-being of their parents. Such children focus a great deal of feeling, energy and behavior on doing "their responsibility".

When these children become adults and develop a relationship with another person, the old family responsibility (responsibility to family of origin) may remain in full force and may even take priority over the well-being of their own partnerships. Family of origin dependency is a very common invader to the intimacy of a coupleship. Comments we hear in this enmeshment are:

"My mother would be so disappointed . . ."
"My father would hit the roof . . ."
"We've just got to go home for the holidays . . ."
"It's always been done that way in my family . . ."
"My father expects our son to be named after his father . . ."

Another complication: In painful families there are subtle efforts to engage grown children in the resolution of the parents' struggles. An alcoholic may marry an overeater, and they will struggle to control each other's addiction, turning to the children to be their allies and supporters.

In the "looking-good family", superficial pleasantness masks deep loneliness and hunger for intimacy between the parents. In very nice ways (and in the absence of an obvious problem), the parents will develop enmeshed relationships with their children and grandchildren, to give their own bleak relationship excitement, pleasure and joy. Children and grandchildren are taught to be grateful and beholding to the very giving and pleasant grandparents — a more subtle form of invasion.

Hidden agendas and covert alliances can turn any prospective coupleship into a complicated nightmare. Both partners need to share with each other what boundaries they want to set with parents (both partners' parents) and all siblings.

Children

It's important for couples to teach their children right from the beginning this over-riding rule: *The coupleship is a bond between the parents that deserves respect and nurture.*

When that concept has not been taught, the children grow up with distorted views of their own importance. As young children and as adults, they grandiosely feel that it is perfectly acceptable for them to interfere in the relationship between the parents. They side with one parent or the other, they make financial and behavior demands on one or both parents, they feel justified in having their needs met, even if it inconveniences the coupleship.

Such children have learned a very destructive lesson: They have learned to think that the children's needs are more sensitive and important than the needs of either parent.

All too often, children are the recipients of attention, focus and touch that partners are hungering for from each other. Daddy's little princess, for example, gets much of the attention and focus that mother needs from daddy. Mother's little sweetheart just as often receives the affection, touch and care that mother needs to be giving her husband.

The child grows up in this kind of family with distorted attitudes and feelings about what they expect and deserve. These distortions prevent the children from being able to have healthy intimate relationships. When they become adults, they are greedy, demanding and unrealistic about their own roles in a coupleship. The parent does the child no favor by giving them excessive love and attention.

In a thriving coupleship children enhance the lives of the parents, and the parents create a loving, learning and healthy atmosphere in which the children grow into adulthood and personal freedom. The consistency of the couple's growth and understanding of each other continues to build an atmosphere of care for the children who pass through the lives of the couple.

Children are, in a sense, visitors in the life of the couple. There will be parts of the following stages (depending on circumstances, birth, adoption, foster care, and so on) . . .

conception and pregnancy
birth and infancy
school years
young adulthood
grandparenting

The Parenting Chart should be filled in with your own personal experience and dates. However, the sample can provide you with an accurate picture of your own coupling and parenting years. In the example above, after a little over 20 years growing up in a family and living as singles, the couple spent approximately 20 years parenting.

If the partners lived until 65, an additional 25 years were spent coupling. Each year would add another year to the coupling portion. With today's longevity standards, the average person might spend approximately 35 to 40 years in the coupling phase of their life. It's clear to see that we should place a high priority and value on the devotion and work that goes into developing and maintaining a passionate and loving relationship.

Notice that there are relatively few years of active parenting in the lifecycle of most couples who have children. Couples who lose their intimacy during these few short years experience deep loss and grief when it is time for the children to move into their own adulthood — the "empty nest syndrome".

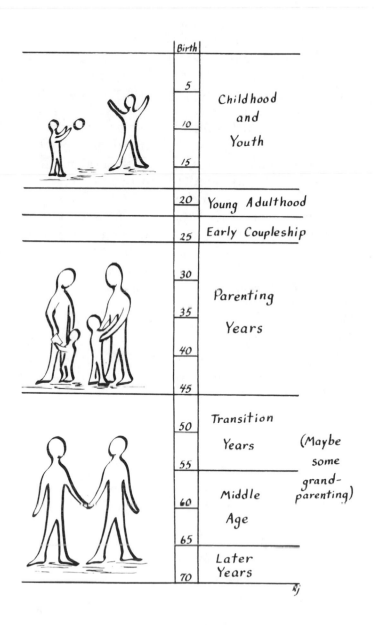

Birth	
5	Childhood
10	and
15	Youth
20	Young Adulthood
25	Early Coupleship
30	Parenting
35	Years
40	
45	
50	Transition
55	Years
60	Middle
65	Age
70	Later Years

(Maybe some grand-parenting)

Parents who devote excessive focus on the lives of their children run the risk of becoming emotional clingers. Rather than experience the joy and fulfillment of the children growing into their freedom and lives of their own, parents emotionally cling to their offspring, relying on children and grandchildren for energy and pleasure. Emotional clingers live with the distorted impression of themselves being "terrific parents and grandparents" and would bristle at the thought of being "emotional clingers", overly dependent on children and grandchildren.

Sometimes a deep family rupture occurs when the children or grandchildren step out in their own maturity and become more independent. Instead of encouraging independence, parents feel abandoned and respond with anger, bitterness, confusion and hurt. Parents, full of their own inadequacy, foster guilt and other bad feelings in their children when they make comments like "After all I've done for you . . . ," or "All the years I sacrificed what I wanted for you." Accusations of ingratitude or neglect lower feelings of self-worth in a child.

A young adult who is not used to personal freedom will begin to feel guilty and retreat back into the role of "child". Fortunately, many young adults find the resources to continue to mature and eventually learn to accept the parents' disapproval.

Support Systems

Support systems can be therapy groups or self-help groups. In recent years there have been many different kinds of support systems developed. If a person uses therapy or self-help groups for personal support, then takes what has been learned and felt in these support groups and brings it back to nourish the coupleship, then the support systems have been very valuable.

However, some people misuse support groups. They turn the support system into an invader who creates distance rather than closeness in the coupleship. This happens when one or both partners make closer and more intimate connections in their support systems than they do with each other.

Whenever an outside person or group has more intimacy with one member of the couple than the partners have with each other, energy is drawn out of the coupleship and distancing occurs. It's very important for couples in support systems to be aware of this danger and talk and share frequently about the dangers. Support systems can be a wonderful enhancement to a coupleship if both work to make it so.

Substance Invaders

Alcohol and Drugs

Alcohol and drugs medicate our feelings, distort and impair our thinking and behavior. Alcohol and other drugs increase susceptibility to accidents and disease and lead to low-level health.

For many people, alcohol or drugs are highly valued because they "love" the way the chemical makes them feel. As I explained in *Learning to Love Yourself*, people continue the use of alcohol or drugs because a love affair has been started. In this kind of "affair", the person feels closer, more warmth and greater need for the drink or the drug than for their partner. In time chemicals become the center of the person's life.

Reliance on chemicals for changes of mood stagnates natural emotional life, and our feelings become increasingly deadened. Without emotional sharing between partners, frequent misunderstandings occur. Intimacy perishes and the coupleship deteriorates. In my book *Another Chance* I have described in detail the "addiction spiral" and the erosion that takes place during the course of chemical dependency.

Alcohol, drugs and prescriptions can be very powerful invaders to a coupleship. My husband, Dr. Joseph Cruse, has written a book called *The Romance* to describe the relationship between a person and the drink or drug. Viewed from this perspective, alcohol and drugs can become a powerful lover in a tight love relationship.

The alcohol or drug does some important things. It . . .

- offers pleasure
- relaxes
- is readily available
- travels easily
- soothes pain and hurt
- covers inadequacy
- boosts self-confidence

The help and pleasure of chemicals can also be given from person to person. However, a chemical relationship for many people is much less threatening than a personal relationship in which there is both give and take.

A chemical relationship is all take. One does not have to give nor does one have to risk rejection. Chemicals can be bought and counted on in a way that relationships cannot.

We have seen that intimacy requires a deep, personal and open sharing of thoughts and emotions. When we medicate ourselves with alcohol or other drugs, our thoughts become distorted and confused. Alcohol and drugs impair our judgment and we no longer think straight. Under the influence, our emotions become blunted or exaggerated. There may be semblances of closeness and intimacy, but drug-affected behavior is not authentic. Under the influence true intimacy is not possible.

Thus, when we feel as though we are losing our partner or when we detect a lack of closeness or intimacy, it is often because we are losing our partner to alcohol or other drugs.

These invaders are the source of much pain and turmoil in the lives of couples. In effect, both partners become focused on the chemical: The user becomes increasingly compulsive in organizing his life around the chemical, and the partner expends much energy in caretaking, protecting, excuse-making, hoping for change and meeting basic survival needs. Obviously, there is little opportunity for partners to grow toward coupleship when chemicals dominate the relationship.

Nicotine Invaders

Smoking cigarettes and marijuana have become major relationship destroyers. They are subtle medicators of the feelings that are necessary to have intimacy.

Intimacy is very threatening to many people. As we have seen, intimacy entails sharing feelings, secrets and vulnerability. Sex is often a wonderful shared experience — until it is over. The afterglow of sex is a very sensitive time. A person who is afraid of closeness will attempt to increase distance and avoid intimacy by smoking a cigarette.

At other times smokers will medicate hurt, loneliness, irritations with nicotine, instead of talking about these feelings with a caring partner. Limited intimacy is available to those who medicate with smoke.

Finally, those who smoke lose touch with their own senses. Smoking impairs taste and smell, and so smokers must have higher levels of stimulation. Smokers are insensitive to the odors they leave behind. They tend to be unaware that smoking contributes to bad breath. They tend to be oblivious to the fact that the odor of stale smoke lingers on the skin and permeates clothes, curtains and furniture. Unaware, smokers appear to be inconsiderate of the feelings and sensitivities of non-smokers.

But even beyond the cosmetic aspects of smoking, smokers have a reduced sexual drive and since smoking lowers the immune system, smokers have more health problems. Smokers are more susceptible to heart and respiratory diseases and run a higher risk of getting cancer.

Rarely is there a divorce that can be specifically tied to smoking. Nevertheless, cigarettes and joints destroy relationships in a quiet, rather friendly way. They medicate the feelings until the emotional life is destroyed.

A sure test of the medicinal capability of smoking is the return of free-floating anxiety as soon as a smoker tries to quit. Over time, the many natural feelings that a couple would share with each other that would resolve conflict and increase intimacy have been medicated away. Eventually, all the connections to those feelings have been forgotten or lost. The smoker just feels numb or blank in regard to many emotional experiences and memories.

In order to recover the connections and the lost intimacy, it will be necessary to stop smoking and let all the old feelings surface. Through exploring all the old anxieties and feelings, it will become possible to revive the feelings of the relationship that have vanished in a cloud of smoke.

In short, it is possible to renew intimacy. By working through feelings of hurt and anger, the couple will be able to rekindle the feelings of trust, hope and sensuality.

There are other benefits in recovery from nicotine addiction. In addition to the emotional closeness that develops in the recovery from nicotine addiction, there are increased feelings of sensuality and sexuality. Both potency and orgasm have the tendency to increase in nicotine recovery. As mentioned earlier, the fulfillment of sexual intercourse most often follows emotional intercourse.

Food

Preoccupation with food (fixing, controlling, selection, requesting, demanding, gorging, binging and purging) can impact relationships in a negative way. Food is always intermingled with interpersonal and emotional experiences. The smells and tastes of foods are strong emotional triggers. We "love" certain foods (ice cream and pizza) or "hate" certain foods (liver and lima beans). Or we "obsess" on health foods (sprouts, carrots and tofu). Each emotion —

love, hate, obsession — carries enormous historical baggage.

There are three major complications with eating disorders:

1. Metabolic alterations caused by the extreme presence or absence of fat.
2. The use of diuretics, diet pills, laxatives and vomiting.
3. The third complication is a major coupleship invader — the numbing of emotional pain, which results in a person not having their emotional self available to them.

It is very difficult for a person with a food disorder to develop the intimacy necessary for coupleship.

Now let's turn to several other groups of invaders: Behavioral invaders, attitudinal invaders and special invaders.

4

Invaders II

Behavioral Invaders

Gambling

Gambling is part of a spending disorder that many people refer to as "green paper" dependency. It includes shopping as a way of relieving stress. In a sense, this behavior — this green paper dependency — is also a medicator, numbing feelings and undermining relationships. Gamblers spend large amounts of money to relieve stress and get pleasure. Too often, however, the relief is only temporary and the pleasure is fitful and fleeting.

When one person excessively spends money, it places increased stress on the other partner to insure that bills get paid. If your financial life is unmanageable, your coupleship faces a serious threat. Financial irresponsibility leads to arguments about priorities and possessions. Both partners feel misunderstood or unappreciated.

Without resolution of these feelings, the relationship becomes filled with bitterness and resentment. The spending partner then spends more — gambles or shops compulsively — to medicate the bitterness and resentment. When both partners are compulsive spenders, the result is always an unmangeable lifestyle.

Green dependency and financial irresponsibility doom virtually all attempts to create a coupleship.

Sexual Acting Out

When feelings are medicated for whatever reason, our sensory self goes to sleep. We are less turned on, less full of passion. With a dulled or diminished sensory system, we find it very difficult to *feel* aroused. Through nicotine, drugs, alcohol, food or work — among other things — our biochemical arousal system becomes sluggish. A sluggish and dulled sensory system makes us unresponsive to normal levels of stimulation. Desire wanes.

The result: Predictable complications and frustrations in the sexual arena. Men with a sluggish and dulled arousal system find that it's difficult to maintain erections or achieve orgasm. Women whose sensory system has been put to sleep become unresponsive and anorgasmic.

Rather than face the personal responsibility of a sluggish sensual and/or sexual system, the person often denies personal responsibility and blames some outside source for their difficulties. Most often the partner gets blamed for not providing enough sexual stimulation.

With a slow and sluggish sensory system, we need a great deal of stimulation to get turned on. The adrenalin rush of seduction, having an affair or multiple sexual partners are ways to artificially stimulate a jaded sensory system. The adrenalin rush is temporary, however, and in order to maintain high levels of stimulation, the anesthetized person must keep changing partners.

Imagine the pain and frustration of a person who has an affair and feels as though sexual relationships outside marriage are the solution to the doldrums. What a disillusionment to find out that the seduction and affair last only as long as the adrenalin rush of newness is present.

Those who sexually act out can create elaborate theories and reasons for their behavior. But seduction, affairs and other forms of sexual acting out indicate an avoidance in confronting and coming to terms with a sluggish sensory system and frozen or fraudulent emotions.

Potency, orgasm and desire are related to personal energy and personal power and are thus personal responsibilities. Potency, orgasm and desire naturally increase in people who become capable of emotional intimacy. We must be friends before we can be full and satisfied lovers. And we must pay closer attention to the ways we mute, dull and anesthetize our own sensory systems.

George Leonard writes brilliantly on the subject of "high monogamy". He says, "Committed love between two people of high esteem is both 'giving love' and being capable of 'receiving love'." When this dynamic duo of giving love and receiving it becomes habitual in the relationship, both people are transformed.

High monogamy, as defined by George Leonard, is a long-term relationship in which both partners are voluntarily committed to erotic exclusivity. High monogamy, then, becomes exciting and full of possibilities.

"The excitement comes not from the discovery of different partners, but with the newness and differentness of a partner who keeps growing and changing." Both partners share a common vision of life's purpose and how to achieve it. Each celebrates and supports the other — not only in low moments, but in high moments as well.

Psychiatrist Herb Otto points out the rewards of a shared vision and commitment: "Only in a continuing relationship is there a possibility for love to become deeper and fuller so that it envelops all of our life." Only a deep relationship offers "the adventure" of uncovering the depth of our love, and height of humanity. It means risking ourselves physically and emotionally, leaving old habit patterns and developing new ones. It means being able to express our desires fully, while remaining considerate and sensitive to the needs of the other. In such a relationship we are aware that partners change at their own rate, and we are unafraid to ask for help when needed.

Workaholism

Workaholism can be found on the job and in the home. Workaholism is first an attitude and then a behavior. First of all, the workaholic believes that work responsibilities are the most important things in the world. Only the workaholic can be the best and most responsible employee, manager, mother, nurse, father and so on. The workaholic sacrifices time, energy and relationships with intimates in order to keep job, contacts, schedules and other job interests front and center.

In the following signs of the workaholic (taken from my book *Learning To Love Yourself*), you will see how the coupleship suffers from this constant frenetic activity. The workaholic . . .

> . . . stays late on the job
> . . . never gets done working in the home
> . . . always works at something on the weekends
> . . . often skips or cuts short vacation time
> . . . has very little time for talking or emotional sharing
> . . . has a mechanical (unrelaxed and unsensual) sex life
> . . . eats fast and does not enjoy leisurely meals
> . . . feels responsible to act on every idea that surfaces
> . . . has difficulty relaxing

Obviously workaholism interferes with coupleship. When the workaholic becomes totally invested in something outside the relationship, as with other invaders, work itself becomes a competing relationship. The pay-offs for a workaholic are . . .

1. The ability to numb and avoid emotion and emotional risks
2. The ability to control people by justifying one's need to work ("After all, who will pay the bills if I don't?")
3. To cover insecurities (work makes one look important)
4. To get thanks and appreciation from others (compensates for lack of love)
5. To be noticed and liked (if there is not enough intimacy at home)
6. Inability to get pleasure from leisure time

So often, I hear someone say, "What good is making a lot of money if we can't enjoy it together?" What seems to have happened for many workaholics is this: In the making of the money, they have lost touch with the partner.

Married to the job or career, the workaholic is in partnership with the busyness of business. The daily calendar fills up with projects, appointments, meetings — places to be, people to see. To-do lists help organize the workaholic's life so that nothing ever gets completed. Certainly nothing personal. Can you imagine a to do list like this:

7 pm . . . Take walk with partner, hold hands, watch sunset
8 pm . . . Share feelings. . . . listen to partner
9 pm . . . Cuddle partner, reassure . . . reaffirm coupleship

Imagine: Three hours spent in communion with your partner — when the reality is that most couples don't get three hours a week together — in *any* form of face-to-face exchange, much less communion.

There are other behavioral invaders that deaden one's ability to feel and express and communicate with each other in a way that builds closeness and intimacy. The three remaining invaders that I see in my therapy work with couples are *excessive exercise, running* and *working out.* The problem is not in the activity itself — running and working out — but rather that the exercise becomes an all-consuming, compulsive activity. (Engrossment in television or preoccupation with sports are also effective ways to keep partners distant from each other.)

In all forms of compulsive behavior, partners medicate their feelings and their vulnerability. The results are predictable: Distance increases between the partners and with time, intimacy and sexual satisfaction diminish.

Attitudinal Invaders

These are attitudes that cause harm to the quality of a coupleship.

Myths

Myths involve beliefs that cause separation and difficulty for many couples. Below I have listed several of the most destructive myths, followed by the facts that get buried and obscured by mythical thinking.

Myth: Women are less interested in sex than men.

Fact: A woman has an infinitely greater physiological capacity to respond to sexual stimulation than a man does. In good health and close emotional connection, women also have equal or more desire for sex. The truth is that women need time and energy. Often sheer exhaustion prevents sexual assertion.

Myth: Husbands and wives should do everything together.

Fact: In a healthy coupleship there will be a majority of time and activities that are shared together. Yet each person will retain some individuality that will enhance their personal growth and fulfill some of their personal needs.

The benefits of some time alone will enhance the quality of what they have to offer the coupleship. In an intimate relationship, the ratio seems to be about 70 to 80% togetherness and 20 to 30% separateness.

Myth: The harder you work at your sex life, the better it will be.

Fact: What actually happens is that the best sex occurs when you are totally involved in the moment with no mental or physical distractions. It's hard to be totally involved in the sexual experience if you are busy thinking about what and how you should be doing what you are doing. Commenting on the prevalent notion of "sex as work", two sociologists observed that "sexual play in marriage has been permeated with dimensions of the work ethic". These dimensions include special techniques, a carefully studied training program, special equipment and attention to scheduled performance. The performance requires mastery and efficiency in order to produce the ultimate sexual product — manufactured mutual orgasms. At the same time, however, we must recognize that sexual behavior can be enhanced: Maggie Scarf recommends that ". . . basic training in the art of the caress ought to be made part of *every* couple's kit bag of basic knowledge about human sexuality."

Myth: It's a partner's job to make the other partner happy and satisfied.

Fact: Too much unhappiness and irritation surfaces in relationships where one partner is waiting for the other person to make them happy. Taking charge of your own gratification and fulfillment increases the possibility that your relationship will be enjoyable and rewarding.

Myth: Independent and strong women make men impotent.

Fact: A healthy man with strong self-esteem finds the most stimulating partner to be the woman who is most active and able to share herself. The woman who is more likely to make her man impotent is the dependent woman who does nothing for herself or for him, other than be available.

Myth: True lovers know each other's needs and thoughts.

Fact: True lovers are not mind readers. This myth is most active in sexual intimacy where a partner feels a reluctance, through shyness, self-consciousness or inhibition, to communicate needs directly. When we fail to convey our needs — our likes and dislikes — partners have to *guess* at what's going on with us. We learn by instruction and by sharing, not by guesswork.

Myth: Time will take care of things.

Fact: Time can be used to resolve conflict, to romance the partner, to try different ways of relating and to build intimacy. These are all pro-active efforts to build a partnership. To do nothing and expect a relationship to grow and flourish and be able to face stresses and strains is a fantasy.

Negativity

This attitudinal invader shows up in people who constantly see themselves and life in a negative way. They work themselves into a state where no one can please them, and they make everyone around them miserable.

When you are in this negative state, you wear yourself out. Your fight-or-flight instincts go into action. Adrenalin flows, pulse quickens and if you stay in this state, the body gets distressed and out of ease. It becomes dis-eased. Negative thinkers often suffer from headaches, ulcers, high blood pressure and many forms of allergies. Negativity is a learned response, a habit we develop over years of taking in the attitudes of the people around us (parents, teachers, friends, co-workers, etc.).

Being in a relationship with a negative person is very difficult. Negativity controls the relationship through exaggeration and blame. Compliments or affirmations are rare. There is a lot of black and white thinking. Either everything is great (seldom) or everything is awful (more often). There seems to be a great deal of tension. Because the negative person jumps to conclusions, the partner becomes careful and secretive to avoid hassles. But the negative person detects the secretiveness and reacts with more negativity. Trust, honesty and pleasure are steadily reduced. Eventually, the tension becomes an insurmountable barrrier to coupleship.

Special Invaders Into Coupleship

Third-Party Affairs

Over the past few years the evidence of increasing infidelity seems unmistakable. There are many reasons. Some of the reasons include:

- Affairs are glamorized through television.
- Both men and women have an opportunity to share meaningful time together in the workplace.
- The availablility of out-of-town travel for both sexes means that many partners get left at home while the other partner is on the road or in the air.
- Greater economic independence gives women more security, making them less willing to put up with an unresponsive mate.

Most people begin a relationship filled with hope and a commitment. They plan to be faithful. However, what people want and hope for is sometimes different from the way they behave when tempted or under stress. Some relationships are more vulnerable to infidelity than others.

In my own work I have observed that affairs tend to take place at maximal stress times. These tend to be birth, death, illness, loss of job, geographical move or retirement. These are times when the power of intimacy can carry someone through. For the couple who has trouble with intimacy, an affair will fill some needs and still allow them to avoid intimacy with their partner. Usually an affair is a sign that both partners are cooperating with each other, obviously or subtly.

To professionals who work with hurting couples, there is no such thing as a wronged spouse. There are only marriages in which there is conflict and pain. One person's unfaithfulness is a manifestation of that conflict. Usually both partners play a role in the situation and both need to help resolve it.

Second Marriages

Ex-partners and all the complications implied often interfere with a newly-formed coupleship in the making. Many second partners soon get discouraged and worn out by working hard to get the approval of the many people who are already involved in their mate's life. Former mates and in-laws add to the conflict — especially where money and time are concerned.

Money demands and obligations from past marriages are often the most effective and convenient methods of control and revenge. By continuing the economic conflicts, there is always a link to the ex-partner.

During the courtship everyone is on good behavior and there is the hope that things will work out. Unfortunately, one of the painful realities following a second marriage is that the couple face a lifetime of strained involvement with the ex-mate (or grown step-children). With the recognition of that reality comes anger, then repression and often depression.

Unless these feelings are shared and truly heard by each partner and a sensitive plan developed, the hurting party may become vulnerable to drinking, drugging, over-working or outside affairs to get temporary relief from the pain and burden. It's important to note that second spouses are naturally and rightfully insecure in their relationships without added pressure, and the added pressure just might make the situation intolerable. Jealousies often arise over the ex-mate and the children from that union. No matter what the source of the jealousy — ex-mate, children, finances — it's important to recognize that jealousy is a perfectly normal outcome of the fear of loss or abandonment, combined with resentment at having to share the present relationship with people from the past.

Resentment builds up because the second mate feels trapped in a highly structured situation they had no part in creating. It seems unfair and impossible to resolve. This pain and this resentment must often be borne alone. The second mate seldom gets support for feelings of anger, hurt or fear about the first and original spouse. Again, sadness and resentment become major invaders in the happiness and fulfillment of a second marriage.

There are many little instances of oversights, choices and decisions that feel like a betrayal to the second spouse. The new partner loves the new mate, but hates the situation. It takes a great deal of energy to live in a constant love/hate situation.

It is important for second mates to give partners permission to like or dislike a new mate's ex-partner and his or her children. Whether the new mate likes or dislikes the former spouse and the step-children depends a great deal on whether the new mate is respected and treated as a valuable choice of their partner. Second mates need to develop their own confidence in themselves and remember that they were chosen.

We all have ideas of what a partnership is but basically it is a choice and a union between two people who care enough about each other to want to make a life together that will offer strength, comfort and joy. In order for this to happen, the legal and spiritual laws have granted a process of coupling that is available to those who choose it. It is the right of each partner to build a life together, regardless of any previous relationship.

> *It is the right of two committed people*
> *to form a relationship and begin to*
> *build a life together.*

Two-Career Marriages

Two-career marriages offer wonderful possibilities for intimacy, sharing and fulfillment. Yet in our work and success-oriented culture, time for the coupleship frequently vanishes.

Traditionally one partner took care of the outside pressures and provided material security. The other took care of home pressures and provided emotional security. Today, both partners are likely to be going full speed in their individual careers and struggling to see that home needs are met. What gets neglected is the time a couple needs to build, nurture and maintain a relationship.

Through work we do a great deal of "doing" and accomplishing. We find a certain identity and we make ends meet. Through partnering, we are more just "being" — allowing ourselves to feel, relate and comfort each other. When work is too major a priority, our sensual and affectionate selves get neglected and often wither away.

A major invader into the two-career marriage is "sexual fatigue". With the adrenalin rush of schedules, deadlines and accomplishments, the surrender to the time and energy it takes to maintain a fulfilling sexual life rarely happens. Instead of facing personal responsibility for the choices of time and energy levels, the partners cite travel, tiredness and demands as the cause of decreased sexual time with each other. There is a common feeling of desertion as each partner begins to feel more and more alone.

Two-career marriages need to take the time to assess and understand the quality of their relationship. If the couple is committed to each other, it is often necessary to make decisions and choices to protect the essence and energy of the partnership.

How are the responsibilities divided? Does the wife who works still maintain primary responsibility for running the household, or does the husband pitch in? When he pitches in, does he really share the duties, or does he do the bare minimum to demonstrate "good faith"? These issues need to be out in the open instead of buried, avoided or ignored because discussion would provoke "too much hassle".

All these invaders need to be faced. There comes a time when couples make a decision to devote time and work on the coupleship. An important truth is that the only way out is through.

> **_The only way out is through._**

Where do we start? We start with talking to each other, listening and sharing concerns in an atmosphere of trust and opennesss, free of blame and animosity. If we are to reach the inner pain, we must be willing to talk and to listen to each other's feelings, hurts, angers and desires. We must strive for clarity and work problems through to the point of understanding and forgiveness.

Easier said than done, but the first step is always the hardest, and practice in sharing and listening makes perfect. It takes raw courage and absolute honesty with self and others. Self-honesty is the conscious effort and clear choice to eliminate games and secrecy from our lives and communicate in that honesty to others.

The 10 Best Ways to Invade, Stifle or Kill a Coupleship

1. Give your mother, father, friend, boss or child more credence and respect than your mate.
2. Schedule your partner's time without first asking.
3. Put your own insecurities and inadequacies on your mate and expect them to be fixed.
4. Insult or put down your mate in public (or private).
5. Add "old" data or anger to a new and current fight, and resurrect old battles and ancient hurts.
6. Talk frequently about an ex-anything.
7. Withhold the sharing of true feelings.
8. Be indecisive.
9. Act fragile, helpless or inept.
10. Tell partial truths.

If two people grow apart (become physically and emotionally distant), it is because one partner refuses to participate in giving the coupleship the attention it needs. Indifference, irresponsibility and neglect doom the coupleship. When one or both partners have no commitment to the quality of their relationship, coupleship will remain unfulfilled.

The next chapter addresses the reality that some relationships will continue to grow deeper and more meaningful and over time some relationships will die.

5

Commitment

To Self and Partner

One does not fall "in" or "out" of love.
One chooses to grow and deepen love,
or one chooses to ignore the needs of love
and love withers and dies . . .

As we examine relationships closely, some couple alliances stand up well. They are founded on the strengths and cooperation of both parties. Friendship and intimacy deepen, and mutual respect and love grow. Partners continue to have trust and openness and express great satisfaction with the union.

Many other relationships, however, consist of what Lederer and Jackson called in *The Mirages of Marriage* a "Gruesome Twosome". The partners may be cordial nodding acquaintances having the same address or they may be combative roommates occupying disputed territory. Gruesome Twosomes do not really like each other. They feel distrust, resentment, frustration with each other.

Intimacy is rare between guarded partners — but there may be a good deal of strained politeness in such a relationship. Partners may be able to keep up a facade of caring and love for political or religious reasons, for the sake of the children or other family members or because they feel there are no alternatives.

Why do we stay in unhappy relationships? Boston College sociologist Diane Vaughan pondered the question after interviewing over a hundred couples who had "uncoupled". Her findings led her to conclude that we hang on to unhappy relationships . . .

- Because we believe in commitment . . .
- Because we feel bound by law . . .
- Because we don't want to hurt the other person . . .
- Because we're insecure . . .
- Because we're not quitters . . .
- Because uncoupling costs money, time, energy and other relationships, and we can't afford to go . . .

"We do it for our children. We do it for our parents. We do it for God." We hang it there because we've learned that's how it's supposed to be.

Prologues to Commitment

So how is it that we find these vast differences among couples? Why is it that some couples seem to click, while others grate on each other like two pieces of sandpaper rubbed together? At least part of the answer lies in the family history of each partner. In her book *Intimate Partners* Maggie Scarf observes:

"When it comes to the forming of adult relationships, we work to some large degree with assumptions that have been made very early in

our own individual histories. For every act of love
in mature life there is a prologue that originated
in infancy: In that time, lost to the mature
person's conscious awareness, when life's first
passionate attachment was slowly forming and
emerging into being."

In that early prologue the first model of later commitments takes shape. Later experiences with our parents
continue to mold our notions of relationships, love and
intimacy, caring and commitment.

Many people who grew up in painful families had very
little appropriate role-modeling or preparation for adulthood. Psychological neglect and physical abuse set the stage
for low self-esteem in youth and later in life as well.
Emotional distance in the family creates children who not
only distrust emotions, but who may come to suppress and
deny emotions altogether.

As children grow they need direction and role modeling
in order to develop their intellectual, physical, spiritual,
behavioral and emotional selves. From their parents kids
also learn ways of handling stress, ways of loving, fighting,
keeping promises, trust and distrust. As children learn to
know themselves in each of these areas, they become more
conscious of themselves, who they are and what they want.
Unfortunately, many children — especially those raised in
troubled families — learn basic rules which numb feeling
and sentiment and prepare youngsters for stunted and
emotionally closed relationships in later life.

Children from damaged families especially get short-
changed in the area of emotional development. They don't
learn the basics of caring and affection. When children see
emotions primarily used to manipulate and intimidate, they
come to fear and distrust their own emotions. Parents who
were medicated, stoic, repressed, depressed or chronically
resentful and angry cannot establish a home life where
children feel free to learn about emotions and come to
understand them. When adults do not understand their own

emotions, they cannot be expected to instruct their children (by example or otherwise) to become open about feelings.

Futility of the Blame Game

As we begin to get a first glimmer of the importance of our early experiences on our later lives, we may have a sudden insight: "My parents are to blame for my inability to form lasting and satisfactory relationships!"

This insight, however, is of limited usefulness, for it primes us to assign blame and takes our attention away from the reality of today's situation. The blame game provides a handy excuse for dwelling in the past and harboring resentments. It also gives us an excuse for not changing our lives in the present, for blaming and feeling righteous and self-justified are much easier than taking steps to change.

The blame game closes us off from compassion for our parents. They had their own individual histories. They were also influenced in childhood and primed for certain kinds of relationships. Given their own models, their own prologue for intimacy, caring and commitment, perhaps they did the best they could under the circumstances. Perhaps parents could not adequately model love because they had been closed off from their own feelings early in life. Perhaps they had never seen a loving relationship and didn't know how to establish one. **You Cannot Give What You Do Not Have.**

You Cannot Give What You Do Not Have

No one has a totally idyllic childhood. No one's parents were perfect. Excavating the past might help us understand the roots of our own troubled relationships, but if we dwell on past injustices — if we grieve them with a vengeance — we run the risk of becoming professional victims. By all means, hold childhood up to the clear light of day, grieve it if you must, but don't wallow in grief — don't become paralyzed by gazing backwards. Getting stuck in the past is a sure way of neglecting the present and sabotaging the future.

Children from troubled families grow up chronologically and physically and begin to make lifestyle decisions (career, marriage, parenting, and so on) without ever fully maturing in the emotional dimension. In a way, many children who grew up in high-stress homes made unconscious lifestyle decisions based on emotional deprivation. They are like sleepwalkers — eyes wide open, apparently aware, but moving in and out of relationships without ever knowing what's going on.

They seek relief for emotional pain by making a relationship only to find that they aren't cured, but merely numbed. Their distress increases more over time. Why does this distress cycle continue? Because painful people attract other painful people and healthy people attract healthy people. Thus, the person in pain increases the pain in marriage because they partner with another person in pain.

Change can occur — even within painful, combative relationships. For example, if one partner chooses to get well and recover (usually following some crisis that initiates attention to the relationship), the critical question will be: "Are both people willing to seek help and make changes?"

In other words: *How strong is the commitment of the partners?*

Leo Buscaglia gauges the strength of a good relationship and the potential destructiveness of not-so-good relationships in his book *Loving Each Other:*

> "The very measure of a good relationship is in how much it encourages optimal intellectual, emotional and spiritual growth. So if a relationship becomes destructive, endangers our human dignity, prevents us from growing, continually depresses and demoralizes us, and we have done everything we can to prevent its failure — then,

unless we are masochists and enjoy misery, we must eventually terminate it."

I've found that about half the time both partners have the commitment to explore the dynamics of the relationship, and half the time the commitment is asymmetrical: One person wants to recover and make necessary choices and changes, but the other partner does not.

Psychiatrist David Viscott once wrote, "There comes a time in some relationships when no matter how sincere the attempt to reconcile the difference or how strong the wish to recreate a part of the past once shared, the struggle becomes so painful that nothing else is felt and the world and all its beauty only add to the discomfort by providing cruel contrast."

A hard truth to meet head on: **Some relationships will flourish and some relationships will have to end.**

Another hard truth: A couple can survive with a one-sided commitment, but the enhanced alliance of coupleship will remain distant, out of grasp.

What is hopeful is that change can always occur with choice. Two people can learn, relearn or unlearn whatever they need to in order to build up the coupleship. Change involves three steps . . .

1. A dissatisfaction with the way things are . . .
2. A decision to make a commitment to the work needed for change . . .
3. A constant dedication to the struggles involved in growth . . .

Two people committed to work together come to realize that deep friendship and passionate connections are needed to go into the adventure of uncovering the depth of love and the peak experience of coupleship. They know that change means risking physically and emotionally, leaving behind old habits and practicing new ones, being willing to risk vulnerability and appearing foolish by expressing true feelings. When the commitment to change is mutual, each person becomes more sensitive to the needs of the other.

Responsibility for these changes can feel like a burden or a giving up of freedom, but the opposite is true. When a commitment to a relationship is made, partners actually become stronger. They acquire two minds instead of one, four hands instead of two. Things actually get easier. There is twice the courage, twice the hope and twice as many possibilities. These are the rewards of coupleship.

When Relationships Change

People change and grow: Some grow together and some grow apart. Not surprisingly, commitment also changes during the course of a couple's alliance. Commitment to the union waxes and wanes. At times it is more intense, at other times there is only a slender thread of commitment. One partner may have a stronger commitment to the relationship than the other partner. And then in time this asymmetrical commitment may reverse. Or it may grow into asymmetrical commitment where both partners feel about equally committed to each other and to the union.

Some marriages do grow in love and vitality.

"Unhappily," writes Carlfred Broderick, "the group that grows is in the minority. Even among marriages that survive the first 20 years, there is a powerful tendency for communication between mates to decline, interests to diverge, mutual criticism to increase and ardor to cool."

Anita and Robert Taylor describe the changes in the course of a relationship in terms of a life cycle:

> "Couples pass, too, through sequential stages, differing from individual and family life cycles in that they reflect the one-to-one relationship. The couple becomes an entity as real as a person or family, and the couple life cycle is separate and distinct from the life stages of its two partners."

The stages are Commitment, Accommodation, Assessment and Recommitment (or Termination). Let's take a closer look at each of these stages in the life cycle of a couple.

- **Commitment:** This is the initial stage where the couple forms pacts together — the overt or covert contracts they make which contain expectancies and responsibilities.
- **Accommodation:** In this stage of the life cycle, the honeymoon is over. The partners begin the sometimes tedious chore of adjustment to each other's flaws and idiosyncrasies.
- **Assessment:** This occurs when the relationship comes under some form of stress, and it's a time when the partnership comes under close scrutiny. It's a period of evaluation where the question inevitably arises: Shall we stay together or not? The costs and benefits of remaining in the relationship are calculated and a decision is reached about the immediate future of the relationship — that is, there is a recommitment or a decision to terminate the union. Obviously, this is the stage at which couple bonds are the weakest.
- **Recommitment (or Termination):** Recommitment is a new affirmation of the couple alliance, a renegotiating of contracts and a mutual decision to continue as a couple. Recommitment, however, does not necessarily mean "until death do us part". New accommodations may not work out. Circumstances may change. And the couple enters once again the stage of Assessment.

All couples pass through the same life stages, some slowly and some more rapidly than others. Some couples pass through the couple life cycle more than once.

The Recommitment may take place by default — not as a result of a strong affirmation, nor as an energetic determination to enhance the relationship. The Recommitment may simply be a decision that it's better to live as a passionless couple than to live as a lonely single. The Recommitment may be a tacit recognition that the economic benefits of remaining together outweigh the psychological gains of termination. Thus couples often remain physically together in a spiritually dead relationship.

Let's look at some characteristics of a spiritually dead and a spiritually growing coupleship. I use the term spiritual because I think it says it best. Spiritual means full of life, full of passion, full of energy. The opposite of spiritual used in this sense is empty of life, passion or energy. The relationship is either alive or dead, regardless of the physical life or death of the parties involved.

Spiritually alive relationships	Spiritually dead relationships
1. High energy and excitement	1. Low energy and sadness
2. Respond to each other's needs	2. Indifference to each other's needs
3. Passionate sexual encounters	3. Passionless sexual encounters
4. High trust level	4. Lack of trust
5. Best friends are each other	5. Best friends outside coupleship
6. Many meaningful talks and sharing true feelings	6. Routine and superficial communication
7. Knows the other, listens and understands	7. Both feel unheard and misunderstood
8. Pleasure in each other's company	8. Grim times together
9. Manageable lifestyle — can say "no" to protect coupleship	9. Busy and chaotic lifestyle — can't say "no" to invaders
10. Plan playtime carefully	10. Not much playtime together
11. Work through conflicts	11. Silent treatment and avoidance

When people's relationships and "spirit" (energy) have
been dead for some time and they have simply avoided
facing the truth, they often deny the seriousness of pain in
the relationship. It's called the "I know, but . . ." syndrome.
It looks like this:

Inside message to self	Outside behavior
1. It's not that bad; it could be worse	1. Do nothing to change; avoid the problems
2. Discount the pain; downplay the hurts	2. Explain or justify the way it is, blaming an outside stress
3. Deny the possibility of change	3. Resist confrontation and play victim. Act self-pitying
4. Ignore one's abilities and personal responsibilities	4. Gets depressed, medicates with excessive behavior (eat, drink, work, etc.)
5. Low self-worth and apathy	5. Addiction, burn-out, depression, suicide

When both partners continue to deny conflict, they may
appear to live in harmony, but each carries their own private
pain. If both partners share the same pattern of denying
reality and make efforts to "look good", the only clue to
their troubled lives will be the painful lives of their children,
who have also been taught to deny reality. The stresses and
strains of living a lie are frequently expressed in the stresses
and strains of the children. Another sign of a "looking good"
painful couple is the stress-related illnesses and chronic
physical problems that seem to plague either or both of
them.

A critical assessment of the satisfaction of each partner is
an absolute necessity to the deepening of a love relationship. It is sometimes frightening to do so as each partner

may feel they are opening up a sharing that may lead to loss of love. Yet if we do not closely examine the quality of our relationship, we forego the possibilities of improving it.

> "Security is mostly a superstition. It does not exist in nature, nor do the children of men as a whole experience it. Avoiding danger is no safer in the long run than outright exposure. Life is either a daring adventure or nothing."
>
> — Helen Keller

In this exploration of coupleship you may find it a bit strange that I am talking of separation, spiritually dead marriages and divorce. It becomes necessary to do so because, as stated earlier, some marriages and relationships will have to end. We know too much today to view divorce as a failure of a relationship. Sometimes a divorce is a recognition of the fact that there never was a conscious choice and never was coupleship.

Let's be frank: Many people would not be married today (or certainly not married to the same partner) if they had it to do over again. Looking back, they can see the truth of the old proverb: "Marry in haste, repent at leisure." They can also see the benefits of more knowledge about relationships, and they are more aware of the extreme importance of clarifying prenuptial assumptions and avoiding secret contracts. Above all, they are in a much better position to appreciate the critical role of friendship between partners.

Many first marriages are an unconscious attempt to heal the emotional pain of hurt, abandonment and loneliness that come from growing up in a troubled family. The partners fervently wish that the new union will make them whole, only to discover that they have recreated havoc and turmoil. Hoping for miracles, they grasped at a relationship and found no miracle, but only a bitter, mundane reality and endless conflict with another fragmented person.

It's no wonder that every 27 seconds someone in this country is getting divorced, adding up to over one million divorces a year. As Carlfred Broderick says, modern marriage is a contact sport:

> "The most popular — and the roughest — contact sport in the country is not professional football; it is marriage. Consider the statistics: Over 90% of us try our hand at it, either ignoring the dangers or simply hoping for the best. A third of us, however, sustain so many injuries that we are willing to suffer the humiliation of divorce to get off the field. Yet the promise, the attractiveness, is so great that 80% of those divorced put themselves back into marriage — most of them within three years."

So we couple, uncouple and couple yet again. That's why it's imperative to learn from separation and divorce, so that the attempt to couple again will be made with much more insight and many more personal assets.

Separation and/or Divorce

If you feel that a separation or divorce may take place, there are some steps to take in preparation.

1. **First of all, get professional help.** Do not make critical lifestyle choices without outside counsel. There may be many opportunities to heal and resolve conflicts with the help of a competent therapist. If it becomes necessary to split, then use that therapist to help you understand yourself and retain your confidence.
2. **Develop a support system.** Often friends and relatives who have known the couple have difficulty being objective during the time of a separation. This

is a time to reach out and take responsibility for forming new friends. There are many groups and self-help programs that can lend support and direction during these difficult times.

3. **Remember your health** and the extra attention you need to give yourself right now. Walk at least two times a day and watch what you eat and drink. This is a demanding time and you deserve to care for yourself the best way you can.

4. **Be able to support yourself.** Think about more education, re-training and part-time work. As you venture into the world as a single person, be able to make your own way in freedom.

5. **Find a skilled and compassionate lawyer.** The best lawyer is one that will want to work with you on being fair and coming through this time with as little trauma as possible.

6. **Begin to dream and plan.** You will be on your own and you will be responsible for yourself. Dwell on the best and the best will begin to happen for you.

There is Life after Divorce . . .

"Pick yourself up, brush yourself off and start all over again" are the words to a famous song and not a bad idea. Building up confidence again may take awhile, but you can make it happen. There are many new goals to make . . .

   . . . finding new friendships as a single person

   . . . taking care of health (exercise, walking, aerobics, diet)

   . . . developing old forgotten talents

   . . . resting and healing

   . . . building employment skills

There are also self-sabotaging behaviors newly separated people are tempted to indulge in. Be aware of the danger and avoid at all costs . . .

   . . . living in the past

   . . . checking up on an ex-mate

. . . trying to get friends to take sides
. . . staying so busy there is no time for self-awareness or feelings
. . . not getting enough sleep
. . . frantically searching for a new love

Take the necessary time to learn from the break-up of a relationship and use this awareness as you prepare to enter another relationship in its due time. Today people who become divorced are not victims. They are architects of a new relationship and a new time.

> *Divorced people can be architects of a new relationship, not victims of the old relationship.*

Remember . . .

If we are to be fully alive, we will live and be a part of change our whole life. Things will not remain static pain or static peace — life is not like that. Life is constantly changing. With change all around, you will have to continue adjusting to the changes. It's a fantastic journey and adventure. Every day is new, every experience is new, celebrate change and get on with it.

Above all: Don't take your partner for granted. Diane Vaughan has studied the process of uncoupling in great detail. Her answer to the question about what works to keep people together: "In a good relationship, negotiation and direct confrontation go on all the time. Whenever one person in a relationship is experiencing some kind of transition — a job change, an illness, a disappointment at work, a death in the family — there is potential stress on the couple. The key is to listen to each other and pay attention to each other's needs, despite any outside distractions. When it comes to the person you love, nothing should be taken for granted."

In the next section, we will explore several case histories of couples who have been able to celebrate the decision to work together to improve their relationship and build a meaningful coupleship. And we will see that some couples needed to end their relationship because they could not continue as mates and partners — could not recommit, and could not make the investment in love, patience and effort necessary to form a coupleship.

No matter which course of action the couple took, the ultimate decision to Recommit or Terminate involved many small choices and many major changes for each partner.

READER/CUSTOMER CARE SURVEY

We care about your opinions! Please take a moment to fill out our online Reader Survey at **http://survey.hcibooks.com**.
As a **"THANK YOU"** you will receive a **VALUABLE INSTANT COUPON** towards future book purchases as well as a **SPECIAL GIFT** available only online! Or, you may mail this card back to us and we will send you a copy of our exciting catalog with your valuable coupon inside.

(PLEASE PRINT IN ALL CAPS)

First Name		MI.	Last Name	

Address			City	

State	Zip	Email:		

1. Gender
- ☐ Female
- ☐ Male

2. Age
- ☐ 8 or younger
- ☐ 9-12
- ☐ 13-16
- ☐ 17-20
- ☐ 21-30
- ☐ 31+

3. Did you receive this book as a gift?
- ☐ Yes
- ☐ No

4. Annual Household Income
- ☐ under $25,000
- ☐ $25,000 - $34,999
- ☐ $35,000 - $49,999
- ☐ $50,000 - $74,999
- ☐ over $75,000

5. What are the ages of the children living in your house
- ☐ 0 - 14
- ☐ 15+

6. Marital Status
- ☐ Single
- ☐ Married
- ☐ Divorced
- ☐ Widowed

7. How did you find out about the book
(please choose one)
- ☐ Recommendation
- ☐ Store Display
- ☐ Online
- ☐ Catalog/Mailing
- ☐ Interview/Review

8. Where do you usually buy books
(please choose one)
- ☐ Bookstore
- ☐ Online
- ☐ Book Club/Mail Order
- ☐ Price Club (Sam's Club, Costco's, etc.)
- ☐ Retail Store (Target, Wal-Mart, etc.)

9. What subject do you enjoy reading about the most
(please choose one)
- ☐ Parenting/Family
- ☐ Relationships
- ☐ Recovery/Addictions
- ☐ Health/Nutrition
- ☐ Christianity
- ☐ Spirituality/Inspiration
- ☐ Business Self-help
- ☐ Women's Issues
- ☐ Sports

10. What attracts you most to a book
(please choose one)
- ☐ Title
- ☐ Cover Design
- ☐ Author
- ☐ Content

TAPE IN MIDDLE; DO NOT STAPLE

BUSINESS REPLY MAIL
FIRST-CLASS MAIL PERMIT NO 45 DEERFIELD BEACH, FL

POSTAGE WILL BE PAID BY ADDRESSEE

Health Communications, Inc.
3201 SW 15th Street
Deerfield Beach FL 33442-9875

FOLD HERE

Comments

6

Case Histories

*People think we are born with the full capacity to
love. They think we fall in love across a crowded
room and it will all work out fabulously. People
have to learn that they have to work at love.*
— *Leo Buscaglia*

Each conflict faced by a couple carries an implied
message: "Stop! Stop living the way you are living. Stop
beating up on each other. Stop taking each other for granted.
Tear away the facade and be who you are."

Counseling can help sort out troubled relationships, but
even the best counseling offers no panacea or instant cure
for every couple in conflict. Counseling may even be seen as
a terrible threat — an ordeal that will pit partner against
partner and destroy the fragile truces and nullify the
unspoken contracts that keep the couple together.

The prospect of change is always threatening. Change jogs
us out of our habitual pathways and makes us uncomfortable. But where there is love and commitment, the

relationship will be strengthened by counseling. Where there is no love and commitment, where there is little consideration and less friendship and respect, therapy cannot create it.

Tom and Diane

Diane starts each day with a cup of coffee and scrutiny of "the calendar". With four children to be chauffeured, fed and managed, she has to pay close attention to the major tasks of planning and coordinating her daily activities. Extra driving trips include track practice, cub scouts, music lessons and soccer games. And almost every day she goes shopping at the mall.

The tennis court where Diane meets her best friend is the only daytime diversion she has from her child-oriented schedule. Her husband Tom is on the road a lot but once a week or so, when he's in town, Diane will plan a dinner or get-together for one of his professional friends. While she always hopes for a time to feel close to Tom and share in his life, she most often gets busy with shopping, preparing food and doing housework.

Yoked to a steady, hectic daily routine, Diane rarely gets a chance to have the intimacy she craves. "We had it once," she recalls wistfully. "We really had it together." But times change, and now she wonders if Tom fully appreciates the time and energy she expends in raising the kids and doing the ever- recurring domestic chores. Does he ever notice her perfectly coiffed hair she has done each week — just to please him? Does Tom pay any attention to her beautifully sculpted nails?

When she finally has time to herself, Diane feels tired and lonely. She feels unappreciated. "I've got to talk with Tom about this," she tells herself. "We've got to get some time together. As soon as he gets home. First thing . . ." Then she drifts off into a fatigued and fretful sleep, setting her internal alarm to rise early because she's got a full schedule again tomorrow.

Alone in a motel room, Tom watches Johnny Carson and pops another antacid. His battle with stomach ulcers is improving, but the memory of a long-term hospitalization last year still clouds the financial picture. The fact that a 60 to 70 hour week led to a seven-week "time-out" for illness is still fresh in his mind. He wonders how do people make it in a regular job? How do people accomplish anything when they work a mere 40 hours a week?

Tom's career has been moving upward for several years. A higher-than-average salary ought to make life easier, yet every month the family ledger shows that Tom and his family are just barely making it — and that's only because Tom travels most of the time and works 60 to 70 hours a week. Car payments, house payments, new addition financing, dental braces, school clothes for the kids, always new and better TV and stereo equipment, credit card payments, club dues — how did it all happen?

Last week Tom joked with one of his friends: "I've got too much plastic. It costs me a thousand dollars just to get out of bed." But it's no joke, and secretly he worries "how do I keep it up?" Much of the time, Tom feels tired and overwhelmed. The last thing he wants when he gets home is another "meaningful discussion" about his relationship with Diane. He also feels unappreciated. Just before he falls asleep, a familiar thought crosses his mind: "I don't understand what's going on with her — I'm doing every-thing I can for Diane and the kids but nobody seems to appreciate it."

Tom and Diane have very little time for their children in a relaxed comfortable way. Most of their contact with them is an "active" or "busy" time. With so little real family connection, both Tom and Diane feel distant and guilty about their relationships with the children and try to make up for the lack of closeness by increasing the things they "do" with each other.

By the time Diane and Tom get together themselves, there is very little *between* them. Both are tired, both feel overwhelmed, both are increasingly irritable, neither have much energy or desire for passion. The passion and closeness they once shared now seems like a luxury or maybe even a little "immature" as the warmth between them has cooled.

The invaders of a "child-centered" upwardly-mobile lifestyle, Diane's "busyness" and Tom's "workaholism" have destroyed much of the possibility of *satisfying coupleship.*

Sue and Ken

Sue and Ken were high-school sweethearts. Being the only boy in a household of women helped Ken feel as though he were special. His mom and his sisters loved making a fuss over him. There was always somebody cheering for him, whether it was in band where he excelled as a cornet player or in the stands when he played basketball. School came easy for Ken and he did well scholastically. Ken felt *very* cared for and loved the attention.

To Sue, Ken looked like Prince Charming. Sue, growing up with several sisters, was "one of the girls". She rarely experienced standing out in a crowd. She and her sisters were reared in a home that taught them to work hard and remember their places as women. (Primary lesson: Women were to take care of men.)

For Ken, Sue seemed like an extension of his home life, an adoring female to take care of him (physically and emotionally). Sue was impressed by Ken's abilities. She thought he looked like a perfect partner. For the first few years the marriage seemed to go well. Ken loved Sue's attentions and Sue loved taking care of Ken.

However, there were soon two children added to the marriage. While the children were very young, it readily became clear that Sue and Ken were not growing toward the kind of intimacy required for coupleship. They had each only extended the roles they knew as children.

Ken felt pangs of jealousy with the births of his own children, rather than the responsibility and protectiveness that a father would feel. He resented the attention Sue gave them. He resented having to work to support them. He became increasingly self centered and self-interested. He took up hobbies and sports that kept him away from home. He spent much-needed family money on his own interests. He looked to his mother and sisters for emotional support and understanding.

Sue reverted to the behavior she knew best. Work harder. She almost single-handedly cared for the home and the children. She became mother, father, homemaker and handyman. At first it felt normal and even good to be such a wonderful wife and mother. However, she became more and more lonely and empty as Ken built a life that didn't include her. She felt the burden of being a single parent, even though she was married.

She began to see that Ken was simply another child to her. The fun they used to have together, he now had with others. Whenever she attempted to talk with him and share her feelings, he would blame her for being boring and controlling. Sue began to resent his boyishness and irresponsibility. And she especially resented his sisters and mother for continuing to treat him like a little boy. Sue found no support in her struggles from her own mom and dad because the relationship she had with Ken closely resembled the family she grew up in. In many ways Ken was just like her father: Distant and cold.

Ken and Sue had come to their marriage as two children. The invaders into their lifestyles were immaturity and irresponsibility. They came together with values and assumptions about roles that prevented the growth of respect and intimacy.

Sue became more and more resentful and finally reached out for help. She went to a counselor, and then to group therapy. Over time she saw her part in the failing relationship. She began to change. At first she became more direct, more assertive. She took a job for two reasons. One was to help with the financial difficulties she and Ken were experiencing and the other was to continue her own growth. She took great satisfaction in her decision to grow up in every area of her life.

However, as Sue changed in a positive direction, Ken regressed, becoming increasingly careless and irresponsible. Eventually he lost his job. Ken and Sue had been growing apart from the instant she took the initiative to seek help. The final split was no surprise because they had been living in separate worlds almost from the start. The major invader was past history — ingrained old habits, unworkable role models, paradigms from the past — encroaching on the present.

Mary and Steve

Mary grew up in an alcoholic family. A first-born child, she was given much family attention and matured very early. It was good that she did because with two alcoholic parents, she was left to care for herself much of the time. Even though she often was showered with attention, she felt lonely, alienated, like a stranger in a strange land.

At an early age Mary started getting involved with people outside her home to fill up the lonely spaces. She joined clubs, took on projects and excelled in most everything she tried. Whe Mary was 17, she was tired, and yet she had found a way to survive: outside validation. She met Steve when she was 18, he seemed a calming influence in her life.

Steve was older, 31. He was a lawyer, quiet, a non-drinker and somewhat of a loner. She loved his quietness, coming from her noisy and often argumentative home. He felt very safe to her. He loved her spirit, her out-goingness and they married within a year of meeting.

The early years of the marriage were calming for Mary. Yet as time went on and as she matured, she yearned for the social life and the connections with people who she had learned to cultivate in her teens. Steve didn't like the social lifestyle, so Mary reached out on her own. She went to school, she played bridge, she joined clubs. The more she joined, the less she was home.

Steve became more and more engrossed in his work and his hobby of computers. He eventually started spending time with a young girl at work who enjoyed his quiet company. They spent quiet evenings walking, talking and, now and then, secretive stolen moments of lovemaking at Marcia's apartment.

Mary's compulsive busyness and Steve's relationship to Marcia eventually became the invaders that severed the slender thread holding Mary and Steve together.

Ann and Jeff

Five years after their marriage, Jeff and Ann were in crisis. The marriage was a second for each. Both had recommitted to this marriage and had great stakes in making it work. However, Jeff was struggling with his grown children from his first marriage. The children did not like Ann and did not want their father to be involved with anyone. Ann was angry and tired of being treated like an outsider in Jeff's family. So much energy had gone into resolving the stepchild issue that there was little energy left to give to their relationship to each other. There were often talks that included blame, sarcasm and belittling.

Jeff and Ann took the first step that led to the preserving of their coupleship. They admitted to each other that they were unhappy and both agreed to get outside help. Their counselor helped them identify their major invaders:

1. Jeff's children (Ann's stepchildren)
2. Their lack of other couples to share with

The counselor wisely taught them about boundaries and how the coupleship needs to be protected and nourished. To protect the coupleship, he taught Jeff and Ann how to present themselves as a couple to the children and give them a choice to accept Jeff and Ann fully as a couple or to reject them as a couple.

Jeff and Ann learned to deal with the stepchildren in a forthright way, saying in words and in behavior: "We are a couple and we will only respond when treated as a couple." This made it clear to his children that there was a new regime.

Things were tense and uncomfortable for a while, but at least all of the cards were on the table. Jeff and Ann had made a decision to protect their marriage.

In time one child accepted them and they have formed a friendship. The other two children are *not* willing to accept them. Both Jeff and Ann needed to have help in making this decision and in accepting the consequences of the decision to stand together as a mutually supportive couple. Jeff needed to grieve the loss of two of his children, he needed to feel and release anger he felt when being judged and not valued by them. Ann needed help to accept the children's rejection of her, her loss of being a stepmom and her anger for the children's invasion of her relationship to Jeff.

After all the feelings were felt and shared, the acceptance of the children's decision grew. Jeff and Ann increased their appreciation of each other and the willingness to work through this issue. The counselor introduced them to some other couples working on similar issues, and Jeff and Ann began making new friends who supported their growing coupleship. Today, there are periodic invaders who try to come between them. However, they have worked hard enough to establish themselves as a couple and invaders just can't get in.

Bill and Kay

Bill and Kay married young. Both had dreams of living the good American life. Bill finished school, got an advanced degree and took a job with much promise. Kay supported Bill emotionally and gave him the three children they both had decided they wanted to have. Both the fourth and fifth children were surprises. Bill's days were filled with work, travel, community and fathering. He wanted the kids to have a very good life, and he saw to it that he took a very active role in their growing-up years. Kay was busy being a single parent when Bill traveled, and then worked hard to reschedule her chores when he was home so he could parent. She used his home time to get caught up on financial paperwork. Both were competent workers, church members, community members and parents. What got lost in the shuffle was "partnering".

There was little time for each other. The result: Both became very lonely. Bill filled his loneliness needs with more work, while Kay found comfort in a glass of wine and a good book.

Crisis came when Bill developed ulcers. Bill and Kay took a good look at their marriage. They spent time talking over what each of them wanted in the relationship, and they made a new commitment to their marriage. It was easy to see what had gone wrong, but it wasn't so easy to fix the coupleship. It took patience and strong determination to do what was necessary to revitalize their marriage.

With the help of some good books, a couples' group and a competent counselor, they got to work.

They started by taking some special time each day and each week for themselves. If Bill was traveling, they connected by phone. Sharing became a priority. They set aside specific time each week to be together, the children were told and taught that they were taking their "partner time" and it was a priority.

Kay began to understand some of Bill's pressures, financial and emotional. She worked with him to develop a budget that would ease his burden and free up some of his time and energy. Bill listened to Kay's cares and concerns. And when she explained that she needed some outside time, he helped her at home so she could enroll in a dance class and college courses.

Both Bill and Kay curtailed community involvement and invested their energy in each other. Their relationship flourished. Both felt better physically and emotionally. Both asked for more from their children and passed on much more responsibility to them. The children balked at first, but soon accepted the unexpected changes with a minimum of grumbling. The coupleship survived and continues in good health.

Jan and Carl

Jan and Carl have been married for several years. They have worked to make their coupleship a healthy and satisfying partnership. But it hasn't always been easy — there were many shaky times, many ups and downs over the years. Carl's job was very demanding and Jan often felt insecure and lonely. Carl loved Jan, but at the same time he felt smothered by her demands for more time than he could give.

Jan and Carl sought help from a marriage counselor and were able to establish a lifestyle that now meets both their needs. Today Jan and Carl are still deeply in love, but don't depend on each other to fill *all* their needs. Let's take a closer look at the accommodation they worked out.

Jan	Carl
1. Jan belongs to a women's group and gets many of her emotional needs met by this group.	1. Carl has a men's group.
2. She likes to keep active and enjoys tennis year around.	2. He likes to hunt and fish.
3. To feel centered and balanced Jan reads a meditation book to start her day.	3. He is active in his church.

4. Jan fills her intellectual needs by reading and taking a night class.

4. Carl works with his computer.

5. She shares an occasional lunch with two close friends.

5. Carl has two co-worker friends, and hunting friends.

6. She has time because she can say "no".

6. Carl can say "no", too.

Jan and Carl have developed a "family of choice". Their family of choice consists of carefully selected friends who respect the coupleship Jan and Carl have worked out.

Note: Their families of choice are not *identical.* Jan and Carl have mutual friends, but Jan and Carl have separate needs and do not insist on doing *everything* as a couple. Jan's women's group, her two close friends, Carl's men's group and his two co-worker friends make up two distinct families of choice who support and care about the individual and the individual's choice of coupleship.

Both Jan and Carl have worked hard to fulfill their own needs so they would have something to bring to the relationship. Once together in a relationship, they have worked to nourish it.

Their friends honor and respect Jan and Carl's coupleship and they as a couple have taught and chosen their family of choice to respect them.

Jean and Don

Jean was a youngest child and only 19 years old when she met Don, 27, and just finishing medical school. Their marriage was a story-book ceremony and their future looked bright. Their first child was born just 11 months later, followed by a second child 11 months after the first.

Don was working long hours, first as an intern and then as a resident physician. As an aspiring "doctor-to-be", he was spared home responsibilities while he concentrated on his studies and his internship. Meanwhile Jean put her own aspirations on the back burner. She took charge of the kids and the household responsibilities. But as the youngest child in her own family she had held few family responsibilities, so she began to feel overwhelmed and trapped.

Jean grew more and more resentful during these early years of marriage. Don, in turn, felt chronically tired and unappreciated. They had a few strong arguments, but weren't able to resolve any of the conflicts and soon found that it was easier to avoid issues, rather than stir up more emotional turmoil. The joy and passion of the union began to dwindle, and they became increasingly formal and distant with each other.

Following the death of her mother, Jean sought counseling. Don was threatened at first, but gave Jean the support she needed to continue. Jean's counselor was quick to see that Jean wanted to deal with some of the issues in her marriage, so Don was drawn into marriage counseling. With some help from a neutral party — the counselor — Don and Jean began to see the brittle unhappiness in their relationship. They began to listen — really listen — to each other for the first time in years.

Jean started to realize that she could get some measure of satisfaction from creating a home without having that be her *sole* purpose in life. She really wanted to go back to school and study for an M.B.A., an area that had always interested her.

In turn Don learned that "fathering" was a neglected part of his role, and once he began to pay attention to fathering, he loved it. He learned to take time off from his formal doctor role and to give more time to the relationships he cherished.

At first, Don and Jean promised themselves a night a week to be alone together and set down some specific times to deal with family issues. But as they grew more accomplished in listening to each other, they became less dependent on scheduled closeness. Their coupleship began to come more naturally.

Marcia and Frank

"I'm really afraid to get involved again," Marcia confided to Frank over coffee one day.

Frank stared into his coffee for a moment. "Yea," he sighed heavily, "I know what you mean."

Marcia and Frank were on their third date and it was obvious that they were attracted to each other. But both had undergone painful divorces and while neither of them relished being single, they had had no desire to jump into a "deeply committed" relationship that might be even more painful than the one they'd just been through with former spouses.

So they carefully felt each other out, talked a lot, spent a lot of time learning about each other's hopes and fears and needs. When they finally decided to get married, they knew what they were getting into. They knew what they wanted in a relationship and spelled it out clearly so there would be no misunderstanding, no hidden agendas.

First of all, they wanted a strong commitment and they wanted an exclusive sexual relationship, with a lot of attention to the "care and feeding" of intimacy. To prevent early disagreements and distrust, they kept much of their life separate. For example, they opened a joint bank account for joint expenses, but also kept separate accounts for their own personal incomes and expense.

Each retained some friendships from their single life to avoid over-dependence on their partner. Each pursued separate hobbies. They even chose to have separate bedrooms for a while.

After two years, their marriage has grown into a strong and clearly defined coupleship. As they find that they want more time together, each of them have begun to relinquish some of their solo pursuits. Yet, Marcia and Frank both maintain a strong sense of identify. They do not smother each other.

When I last spoke with them, they were in the process of remodeling the two bedrooms, turning them into a master suite with a small adjoining library. It was clear that Marcia and Frank were well-rewarded by moving with caution and good judgment into second marriage. They moved slowly, listened, learned about each other's needs and individual style. And they have found that it's never too late for coupleship.

Remember this: Coupleship is a choice, not an automatic happening with promises and vows. It requires work, choice, commitment and love for self and other.

Those seeking coupleship will contribute time, energy and money to the care and maintenance of the coupleship. There will be a need for much sharing, much negotiating, planning and compromising to make it all work out for each and for both. The rewards are inner peace and comfort, a sense of importance and belonging, and unequaled fulfillment.

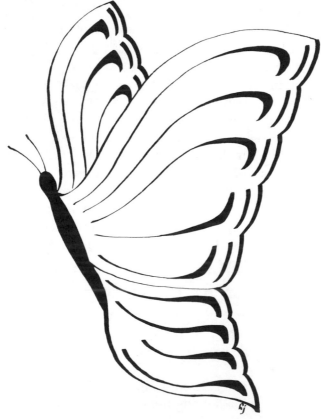

Introduction to The Coupleship Enhancers' Cookbook

This section is written for those who:

... *want to explore new ways to enhance their relationship and find more intimacy and pleasure*

... *want to commit to a relationship but are unsure of what that means*

... *want to put excitement and passion back into a failing relationship*

... *and for anyone else who is interested in intimacy, relationships and romance.*

The suggestions and tools described in Part 2 are used in our five-day intensive coupleship workshops (see Appendix). We have found these tools to be very helpful to couples dedicated to revitalizing the coupleship. I encourage you to try them out with your partner or if you are a counselor, suggest them to clients. In coupleship, as in all worthy endeavors, practice makes perfect.

Enhancing a Relationship

Grant that we may not so much seek to be
consoled as to console
To be understood, as to understand
To be loved, as to love
For it is in the giving that we receive.
— *Prayer of St. Francis*

Many of my patients and clients over the years have said to me, "Sharon, no one ever taught me how to have a relationship. They taught me how to read, work, cook, repair a car, go to school, say my prayers and how to have sex. *No one* taught me how to have a relationship and develop a meaningful, growing, changing and fulfilling coupleship."

No One Taught Me How To Have a Relationship

The rest of this book will be filled with tools, ideas and exercises that can be used to build intimacy, sharing and closeness between partners.

Suggestion: Read all the way through Part II to get a feel for the material. Then come back and work on each idea at a separate time. There is no "best" place to begin. Some of the ideas can be grasped and put to work immediately. Other exercises will take more thought, more practice and repetition.

Remember: It won't do just to *think* about the suggested exercises — although thinking about them is an important beginning. In order to enhance a relationship, eventually these exercises must be put into action. As psychiatrist David Viscott wrote in *How To Live With Another Person:*

> "Relationships seldom die because they suddenly have no life left in them. They wither slowly, either because people do not understand how much or what kind of upkeep, time, work, love and caring they require or because people are too lazy or afraid to try. A relationship is a living thing. It needs and benefits from the same attention to detail that an artist lavishes on his art."

Family Map-Sharing

Do partners have a clear understanding of each other's family history? Many couples have found a sense of enlightenment and a new closeness by taking the time to understand each other in the context of their separate family histories. What were the kinship patterns in immediate families?

Our only guarantee in life is that there are absolutely no guarantees.

In the families of parents and grandparents? Do these kinship patterns suggest ways in which distant relatives and more immediate family members learned to grow and deal with relationships?

Let's take a look at the Family Map of Linda and Ray:
Going back to the grandparents, there were . . .

FAMILY 1

Mathews	Martin		Mason	Buskin
Carl Megan	Don Liz		Henry Rose	Oscar Mabel
Carl II	Nathaniel		Ann	Thomas
	Ronald		Joseph	William
	Stephen		Henry	Caroline
	Jane		Ed	

FAMILY 2

	Mathews		Mason
	Carl II Jane		Ed Caroline
	Carl III		Ray
	Bill		Warren
	Mark		
	Ted		
	Linda		

FAMILY 3

Mason

Linda Ray

etc.

A brief glance at the bare skeleton of the family map gives
strong clues about past family relationships:

1. Linda's mom, Jane, came from a family of boys. She
   might not have had much experience with raising a
   girl.
2. Linda, a last child and only daughter, was probably
   very special — or (perhaps) could have been an
   afterthought.

3. Carl III is a first-born son of a father who was an only child. There were likely strong expectations of Carl and strong family values.

4. Carl III, as a first-born son, might have had a dominant personality, while Jane, being last born, might be more passive.

5. Linda might bring to the relationship preconceived ideas about males and a preconceived notion of the role of women in a relationship.

6. Ray is a first-born with two parents who were both youngest children. Because younger children have not always been encouraged to be strong leaders, Ray may find himself often taking care of his parents — and literally adopting a caretaking role toward others.

7. There are fewer women in Ray's family, so he might not have a had a great deal of experience with relating to women. We would have to know more about his relationship with his grandmothers.

8. Ray and Linda may have some things to work out just in sharing who they are, where the lacks are and how to resolve dominance issues.

By filling in other aspects of the Family Map, other new and informative features of family history come to light. Partners are encouraged to fill in . . .

- deaths
- drinking/drug problems
- illnesses (stroke, cancer, etc.)
- financial ups and downs
- educational attainments
- patterns of defiance and conformity

The more information, the greater are the chances of gaining increased understanding about each partner.

Romance Responsibility

The responsibility to add and deepen romance in the coupleship requires equal effort by each partner. One way to warm up your relationship is with a wonderful and unexpected gift for your partner. Take a basket with a cheery fabric and begin. Here's a few "starter" ideas for gifts to put in the basket:

- Satin sheets
- A postcard of a far away place and tickets to get there
- Home made favorite foods
- A bottle of sand and an invitation to walk along the beach
- Scented oil for a massage
- A scrapbook of favorite pictures
- A "Christmas present" any day of the year
- A calendar marked with special memories or events
- A menu from his/her favorite restaurant and an invitation to go there
- A scented candle and good book for a rainy or snowy night
- Freshly ground coffee, two new cups with special messages and chocolate chip cookies
- Scented bubble bath and an invitation to share a bathtub

There may be a special gift that only you know your partner would appreciate. Spend some time thinking about your special surprise. Or be spontaneous. Give a single gift, or give several at a time for a special occasion.

There is no "correct" way to do this exercise — the important thing is to do it — because it means you are giving your partner special attention and not taking your relationship for granted.

More ways of taking responsibility for romance:

Plan a Month of Romantic Overtures:

Day

1   Hug your partner
2   Pray together
3   Give a compliment
4   Say "I love you" at a special time
5   Go on a picnic or out to a quiet dinner for two
6   Spend one hour on a special hobby or talent
7   Say a prayer of gratitude
8   Have breakfast in bed together
        (Or: Serve your partner breakfast in bed)
9   Get a haircut and spruce up
10 Tell your partner (in words or deeds) "I appreciate you"

11   *Buy flowers for your partner*

12   *Buy a present for yourself and tell yourself that you are neat*

13   *Volunteer some of your precious time for someone else*

14   *Tell someone you are sorry*

15   *Do a favor for someone anonymously*

16   *Listen to a favorite song and let your thoughts flow*

17   *Take a sunrise walk with your partner*

18   *Have a special meal with special food*

19   *Call someone you and your partner care about long distance*

20   *Pay attention to the sky*

21   *Try and tell a joke or an old anecdote from your growing-up years*

22   *Admit that you are sometimes afraid and tell your partner why*

23   *Find humor in everything that happens today*

24   *No matter what is happening, take time to cuddle up to your partner and share what's on your mind*

25   *Tell your partner that you are interested and encourage your partner to tell you what is on his or her mind today*

26   *Call someone locally who is important to both you and your partner and tell him or her just that*

27   *Write a love note to your partner and share a special memory*

28   *Go for a long walk and talk about the first year you spent together*

29   *Pick a romantic place for dinner and talk about how you would like things to be ten years from now*

30   *Pick a movie, eat popcorn and Milkduds and hold hands*

31   *Sit outside for half an hour after dark and look at stars*

Learn How To Fight Fair

Love rarely remains all flowers and sweetness. Disagreements, arguments and fighting are a natural when two people are trying to put together two approaches to life. More important than what you fight about is how you fight together. Your style of combat and resolving conflict can mean the difference between whether you remain a committed couple or break up. Learning how to fight fair is one of the most important lessons you can have.

1. **First, give yourself permission to fight.** Accept that disagreements and fights are natural when two people are trying to merge into a mutually compatible lifestyle.
2. **Know why you are fighting.** Be sure that what you fight about is really what you are angry about. Be honest.
3. **Establish a goal when you fight.** Be sure that you don't fight to win but to clear the air, find a solution, share feelings, gain greater understanding of each other and find a way for both to win.
4. **Fight according to fair rules.** Don't bring up old rules that have nothing to do with the current disagreement. Try not to be hurting, sarcastic or belittling. Stick to the issue and try to resolve it in a way that will bring you closer. Never, *never* hit your partner or try to make a point physically by pushing, kicking or some other form of aggressive contact. Coupleship can survive harsh words, but not physical abuse.
5. **Take responsibility for your own assertion.** Be clear about how you feel and think, and take responsibility for sharing both ideas and feelings with your partner. Confusion complicates understanding. Acting passive often increases problems because one is waiting for something outside of personal effort and risk to resolve issues. Rarely does that happen.

Being assertive means being clear, direct and open about your feelings and desires. It also means being respectful of your rights and the rights of others. Basically, it means functioning at your most honest level.

6. **Show mutual respect.** Don't blame, accuse, demean or insult. Don't try to determine who is right or wrong. Listen with care. Seek to understand and respect each other's point of view.

7. **Pinpoint the real issue.** Often we have "surface" fights that don't touch the basic issue. Feeling unfairly treated, feeling your judgment questioned and resenting it, or feeling vengeful and needing to retaliate may be the real basic issue. Look for what the conflict is *really* about; that's what has to be resolved.

8. **Seek areas of agreement.** When two people are very angry with each other, they often think there's absolutely nothing they agree on. They try to prove each other wrong. But most couples agree on a lot more than they disagree on. Find areas of agreement, even if it is only that you don't want a permanent break. Using that as a springboard, you'll find lots of other things to agree on.

9. **Participate mutually in finding a solution.** Since the conflict involves both of you, it is most helpful if you both seek possible solutions. If both parties offer suggestions on ways to improve things, they have the best chance of reaching an agreement.

Living with and loving someone who doesn't fight fair can be a terrible burden for the other person. Absorb the rules of decent dissension before you and your partner quarrel again. You'll not only fight more constructively, but you'll move on to a happier, healthier outcome.

Repairing Hurt Feelings

Once the fight has ended, it's time to replenish the coupleship and repair the hurt feelings that remain. Fights are like "emotional surgeries" and it is necessary for healing to take place at the closure of the fight. There are three basic ways to approach the healing process:

1. **Apologize.** The apology is only for the parts of the sharing that might be perceived as "not fair" or "not honest". It sets up the fact that while clearing the air and negotiating were absolutely necessary, sometimes in the heat of feelings some transgressions were made.

2. **Assure.** When you have been through difficult times together, it is important to assure your partner that you love, respect and support them, even if you both feel very different about a specific issue.

3. **Accept.** Accept that your partner may be different. Hear your partner's explanations, feelings and ideas. Acknowledge the similarities and differences between you. Accept that there may be more time needed for full understanding, but accept the current status. No one has to be a total winner or loser.

> *"Two people should allow confrontations to take place as painlessly as possible in order to realign both partners' sense of reality, to share the meaning of each other's view of the world, to lay the groundwork for growth within a framework of trust, and to permit both to say 'I was wrong' without fear of being laughed at or taken advantage of."*
> *— David Viscott*

10 Thoughts on Wisdom

1. It is never being too old to hold hands.
2. It is remembering to say "I love you" at least once each day.
3. It is never going to sleep angry.
4. It is at no time taking the other for granted.
5. It is forming a circle of love that gathers in others.
6. It is doing things for each other, not in the attitude of duty or sacrifice, but in the joy of giving.
7. It is speaking words of appreciation and demonstrating gratitude in thoughtful ways.
8. It is in not expecting perfection. It is cultivating flexibility, patience, understanding and a sense of humor.
9. It is the capacity to forgive and forget.
10. It is giving each other an atmosphere in which each can grow.

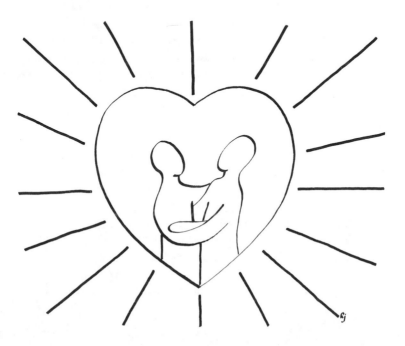

Sexual Closeness

In a coupleship partners learn more about each other's sexuality. We all have varied feelings about sexual contact. Some people are very "underexplored". Sex has been a routine and simple contact. There has been very little time spent finding out what the sexual pleasures of each partner means.

Now is the time to *ask*, time to *experiment*, time to be explicit about your wants and needs. Now is the time to find out what sexually pleases your partner.

It is important! Pleasure in sex is important to human life. Sexual pleasure is not a luxury, but a profound psychological need. In order to live fully, we must experiment to discover our optimum level of sexual enjoyment and we must understand the sexuality of our partner.

The ultimate sexual experience gives us two very important experiences:

1. It allows us to have an intensely vital experience that affirms the value of our coupleship, and . . .
2. It reinforces the sense that we are special individuals in a mutually caring relationship.

The pleasure and joy of sex provide us with the kind of direct experience that is both life- and self-affirming. The intimacy of sex is unique because it is an integration of body, mind, emotions and spirit. When this integration occurs, sex is *the ultimate intimacy.*

With the potential of being an *ultimate intimacy,* it is clear to see the waste and ridicule of only connecting at any one of the connectors (body, mind, emotions and spirit). We cheat ourselves when we settle for anything less than total sharing.

To accept and acknowledge how important sex is to a relationship is a first step in placing value on one's sex life. Sexual activity is healthy. It releases endorphins — the morphine-like substances in the brain that cause pleasure sensations and relieves pain. Sex exercises the muscles, and it allows for a loving exchange.

The following sexual guidelines may be helpful:
1. Pay attention to sex.
2. Make time for sex.
3. Communicate about sex to your partner.
4. Continue to romance and court each other.
5. Give each other positive love messages.
6. Tune in and take responsibility for your own sexuality.
7. Recognize sexual apathy and talk about it.
8. Guard against boring routines.
9. Share your feelings.
10. Be as attractive and as inviting as possible to your mate.

Sharing Time

About every six months, take extra time for the couple ship. Taking time isn't always easy. Schedules interfere. Jobs, kids, money — all can be real reasons why couples find it hard to get private time together. But time together apart from other responsibilities can be a way to renew your friendship and enhance your relationship.

Some folks can arrange to take a weekend and go to a lodge or a favorite resort. Other couples feel lucky if they can just squeeze the time out of a hectic lifestyle by closing the door to their room for a couple of nights and letting the family know *"It's coupleship time"*.

Don't make it too complicated, and don't turn it into an onerous task. Again, this is a way of giving each other special attention. This time together fosters and builds increased understanding, sharing and intimacy.

A special setting can be very important. Perhaps some refreshments, special snack and a lighted candle — anything to help to create a romantic atmosphere. (It's better to avoid alcohol on these occasions, because it tends to numb both thought and emotions.) Some of my clients have told me that they have purchased a very special candle and it is lit *only* when special sharing time is going on.

The partners agree that this is a private session, meant to bring them closer together. There is no hurry; there are no expectations and no goals. Rather than race through many questions to reach a goal, the goal is simply to set a time limit (one hour, three hours, a weekend). The amount of time is less important that the quality of the time spent — the idea of taking some special focused time to pay attention to the coupleship.

This coupleship time may seem awkward at first. Couples may even get anxious about being together without the distractions they're used to. "What do we talk about?"

It may help to do a kind of sentence-completion game: Making time available as often as possible, the couple takes turns going through the following questions. One shares and then the other shares. When the time is up, they put the questions aside until the next time they are able to do some more sharing. Here are some examples couples use to stimulate sharing time:

(Take turns completing each sentence.)
1. Marriage and commitment means . . .
2. When I was young, I thought love was . . .
3. When it comes to sex, what I believe is . . .
4. The difference between me single and me now is that . . .
5. When I think about God or a Higher Power, I . . .
6. Between you and me, what disappoints me most is . . .
7. If I had it to do over in life, what I would change is . . .
8. The way children affect me and you is . . .
9. The hardest part of how my parents felt is . . .
10. The biggest difference between me and you is . . .
11. I'm most apt to cry when . . .
12. When it comes to sharing feelings, I . . .
13. To me, home means . . .
14. I feel most misunderstood when . . .
15. What I hope for me and you is . . .
16. What frightens me most is . . .
17. What I most need from you is . . .
18. When you and I came together, I thought . . .
19. What I wasn't prepared for when we came together was . . .
20. The qualities I love most about myself are . . .
21. The qualities I love most about you are . . .
22. I feel most intimate with you when . . .
23. What I like most about my body is . . .
24. What I like most about your body is . . .
25. I love you because . . .

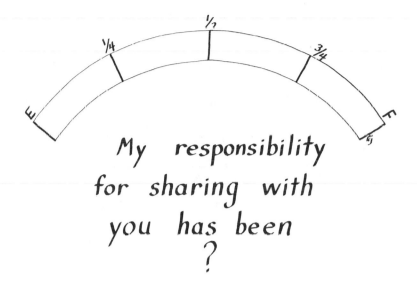

My responsibility
for sharing with
you has been
?

Happy Hour

Happy hour is that time of day when people connect. I refer to this time as re-entry time. Sometimes it is not the end of the day, but rather the coming together after a short or lengthy separation. It may be as one or other partner returns from a trip. Happy hour is the time when two people in "coupleship" have been separated and they need to re-establish their coupleship. Each shares with the other what has happened since they were together. Sometimes this means events, sometimes it means feelings and sometimes it means ideas. What is important is that each expands the world of the other by sharing experience.

In my experience, in order to preserve the strength and connection between two people, it takes about one-half hour per day for this re-entry to take place. When couples are together, re-entry takes place face to face. When separated, couples can have a sense of re-entry or a happy hour with a telephone call or a letter.

After a physical geographical separation, couples need to take at least an hour for re-entry upon seeing each other again. This is important to keep in mind: Re-entry time does *not* include catching up on mail and phone calls or tending to household tasks. Re-entry means focusing on the other and reconnecting, nurturing the coupleship.

Timeless Time

Timeless time is time a couple sets aside to allow spontaneity to occur. Timeless time has no agenda. It allows thoughts to flow freely, it allows feelings to surface and it gives each person the opportunity to be able to recapture a sense of being carefree and spontaneously responsive to each other.

Many have lost the ability to know how to respond openly and freely because they have been programmed with "Proper and Correct" ways to behave. While each of us needs timeless time as individuals to discover our ability to respond, we also need that time as couples. It is the "coupleship" that I am addressing right now.

To insure rediscovery of our ability to respond to each other, it is important to have timeless time — totally unscheduled time — to see what happens. I recommend:

One hour a day . . .

One day a week . . .

One weekend a month . . .

One week each six months . . .

. . . Just be together and see what happens!!!

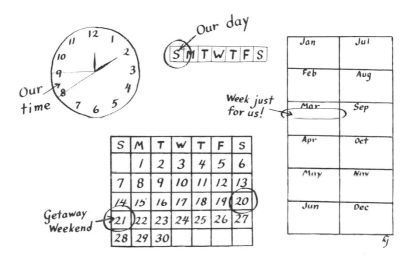

Assertion Philosophy

To become assertive is to take responsibility for a relationship. Recognize some of the characteristics of assertion philosophy . . .

1. Each and every human being is entitled to dignity, respect and courtesy.
2. Human adjustment requires that you stand up for your rights.
3. By not standing up for your rights, you are encouraging the other person to continue treating you in the same unpleasant way by reinforcing his behavior.
4. If you don't exercise your rights, you cannot rationally resent people who do.
5. By not expressing yourself, you may be allowing things to build up inside which may result in an inappropriate and hurtful response later.
6. As stated by Albert Ellis: "It is unavoidable and undesirable to live your life without hurting someone."
7. As stated by Jourard: "Being polite out of fear of being offensive and hiding one's discontent with the situation or the behavior of the other, is a sure way of either destroying a relationship or of preventing one from really forming."
8. Not letting the other know how you feel and what you think is a form of selfishness.
9. If you don't tell someone what you think, you deny them the opportunity to change.
10. Each person has a right to express himself as long as the rights of others are not violated.
11. Mentally healthy people stand up for their rights; do not suffer from the "tyranny of the shoulds".

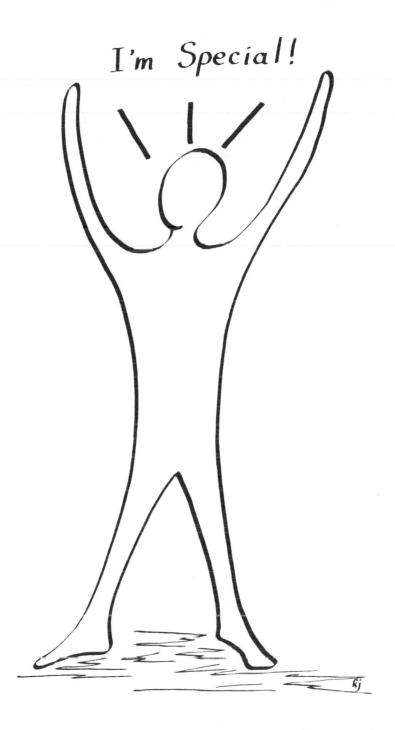

Listening

Over the years, a consistent complaint I have heard from couples is "I feel misunderstood. If only my loved one would listen to me." We have all wished to be listened to. In coupleship workshops and seminars I have used the following meditation by Ralph Roughton on listening:

On Listening

When I ask you to listen to me
    and you start giving advice
    you have not done what I asked.

When I ask you to listen to me
    and you begin to tell me why I shouldn't feel that way, you are trampling on my feelings.

When I ask you to listen to me
    and you feel you have to do something to solve my problems, you have failed me, strange as that may seem.

Listen! All I ask is that you listen.
    not talk or do — just hear me.

When you do something for me that I can and need to do for myself, you contribute to my fear and inadequacy.

And I can do for myself; I'm not helpless.
    Maybe discouraged and faltering, but not helpless.

But when you accept as a simple fact that I do feel what I feel, no matter how irrational, then I quit trying to convince you and get about the business of understanding what's behind this irrational feeling. And when that's clear, the answers are obvious and I don't need advice.

Irrational feelings make sense when we understand what's behind them.

Perhaps that's why prayer works sometimes for some people . . . because God is mute, and He or She doesn't give advice or try to fix things. God just listens and lets you work it out for yourself.

So, please listen and just hear me. And, if you want to talk, wait a minute for your turn, and I'll listen to you.

Commitment

. . . Promise	. . . Assurance
. . . Truth	. . . Understanding
. . . Word of Honor	. . . Agreement
. . . Trust	. . . Pact

Any coupleship that makes it — any couple alliance that flowers into a thriving coupleship — does so because two people have made a commitment. The committed person is one who trusts and can be trusted. For the committed person the thrill of the chase has paled by comparison with the pleasure of a solidly-grounded partnership with one cherished person. To be more specific, I believe that a *sexually exclusive* relationship is essential to a vital coupleship.

Too often, the fantasy of sexual freedom is filled with the reality of loneliness. Trapped by myth and by unreal images, the noncommitted experimenter becomes prisoner of an attitude. When a person expresses a yearning for a warm, loving relationship and is still drawn to one-night stands and short-lived affairs, it is reasonable to ask whether that yearning is real and whether that person is in touch with their deepest needs.

Looks, status, money, hobbies, intellect and other attributes are all attractive characteristics in a partner. But the crucial qualities are character, honesty, integrity, moral courage, humor and a powerful capacity for affection and love.

For the couples able to commit to each other, passion becomes like a flame, fanned by each decision to recommit. This passion is fueled by making a decision to explore, support and love the life of another soul.

We do not feel less free because of commitment. We feel more free because we have made a free choice to commit. Our partnership becomes a liberation and becomes increasingly fun. Our partner makes us feel more capable, not captured. Our partner makes us feel stronger than when alone. Our partner becomes a friend, and without our friend and partner, the world seems bland and ordinary.

A person who strengthens and enhances you, loves you for both your strength and weakness — such a person evokes a love that becomes vital. Feeling that kind of love encourages you in turn to act like a loved person, and in that way you grow and expand to your potential.

The chances of a relationship working depend upon the degree of emotional stability and maturity of both partners. You have to work for fulfillment. It's not a gift. Dreaming makes us lazy. You need to work on yourself before starting a relationship, then work for a relationship that can stand the test of time. A good relationship requires a balance between forgoing and granting, between restrictions and freedom, between feeling a loss of control over yourself and needing control of others, giving tender affection and being appropriately assertive when hurt. It is the pleasure of knowing you are both *reunited*, happily on a daily basis.

Holiday Happiness

Many otherwise happy relationships have difficult times around traditions and holidays.

Somewhere in each of our minds is an image of the perfect holiday celebration. That image might come from stories, pictures, movies or even television commercials. It is likely to include smiling, happy family members gathered together in a cozy setting — usually Grandma and Grandpa's house. They talk and laugh, share memories and intimate conversation, exchange gifts that are exactly what each of them wanted, eat a delicious dinner with all the trimmings, sing carols and have a warm wonderful time together.

For many families, the reality of holiday celebrations falls far short of this perfect image. Family get-togethers of real ordinary people who argue, get annoyed with one another and have different ideas about what's fun don't quite fit the picture of the ideal celebration.

For some couples the holiday reality is so painful and far from perfection as to be a crisis, rather than a celebration. It may be because Grandpa is drunk and abusive at the holiday dinner table. Perhaps a long-standing rift between two sisters erupts in a shouting match that draws other family members in on both sides. Maybe eight-year-old Jason spends the day in tears, because Mom completely forgot that she had promised Santa would bring him the new bike he desperately wanted.

For couples like these the holiday observance disintegrates into just one more unhappy occasion. Instead of carols, there are quarrels. Instead of love and laughter, there are tears and tension. Instead of holiday joy, there is disappointment and sadness.

The stresses of the holdiay season aggravate tensions for any family, troubled or not troubled. It is a time of hectic holiday schedules, too much travel in a short period of time, trying to find enough money to provide the special gifts family members would like, deciding which relatives to spend time with and often having too many people crowded under one roof. All of these help create a climate where tempers and feelings flare.

Often when family members get together, "manageable" issues such as different beliefs in religion, child-rearing and money management come to the surface. Some families also have issues that are less manageable. These might involve second marriages, stepchildren or abuse of alcohol, drugs, money or food. When these issues surface, the holiday get-togethers become a ripe context for crisis.

In painful families that potential for crisis is magnified at holiday parties. Schedules and stresses combine to make it easy for the practicing alcoholic to drink and the recovering alcoholic to slip. The same stresses also provide many opportunities for co-dependents or adult children to disregard their programs of recovery. Relapses often occur during this season.

For the painful family the season is one of an "addiction to hope". Each holiday period offers the possibility that maybe this time things will be different; maybe this year will be better. Despite past celebrations that were marred by drinking, quarrels and disappointments, there is still the hope that "this time it will turn out right". This hope produces unreal expectations which result in painful disappointments. Because, once again, the celebration wasn't "right", family members are left with increased feelings of inadequacy.

Adults who have grown up in painful families often expect themselves to give to their children what they did not receive as a child. They try to create the perfect holidays that are missing in their own childhood. But because they've never learned how to make that kind of holiday celebration, the attempt often falls short. Again they feel inadequate.

They are often torn between the past and the present. They know they need to give time and attention to current situations and relationships, but they are still tangled in past resentments and painful memories. Those memories surface strongly at holiday time, brought out by family gatherings and traditions. They get in the way of enjoying what should be a happy time in the here and now. This produces guilt.

One result of that guilt may be reckless over-spending on gifts to make up for real or perceived neglect of family members in other ways. The over-spending creates a financial burden that adds to the holiday stresses, causing still more feelings of guilt and inadequacy.

So the cycle continues and builds, getting more painful every year.

For the couple trying to find a coupleship, it is necessary to slow down or stop that holiday cycle of pain. It isn't easy, but can be done. The following suggestions offer some ways to begin making changes.

1. **First of all, it is important to reduce your expectations of the holiday season.** Even for healthy families, there are stresses and disagreements at holiday celebrations and family gatherings. Each family needs to learn to measure its situation against the reality of the fact, rather than against an ideal "perfect" family or "perfect" holiday that doesn't exist.

2. **Learn to take the risk of starting new traditions.** Observing holidays exactly the way your parents and grandparents have always done can keep you focusing on the past instead of the present. If those observances were part of a painful situation, they may be empty and meaningless or even full of hurt, rather than pleasure. As an adult you have the right to begin your own traditions with your own children.

   Perhaps it might be more meaningful for you and your partner to take a holiday trip than to exchange the customary gifts. Maybe all of you might decide to spend part of the holiday quietly at home instead of joining a big family gathering. Taking the lead in beginning new, meaningful traditions can be exciting and rewarding. You may even find that other relatives locked into the same hollow observations will be relieved at having you help break that pattern.

3. **Keep some traditions.** Starting new traditions doesn't mean throwing out wholesale every holiday observance you've ever practiced. It does mean taking a look at the ones you still carry out. Why do you do them? Do you bake dozens of decorated cookies because your mother always did, or do you spend that time because you enjoy it? Is sending holiday cards a tiresome chore, or is it a pleasant way for you to keep in touch with friends? Do you decorate your house because it is fun and makes you feel surrounded by holiday spirit, or do you put up displays because everyone else in the neighborhood does and you need to keep up?

4. **Decide as a couple what you want the holiday season to mean.** Is it a time for festivities and celebrations? For church-going and reflection? For sharing gifts? For charity? Remember that there is no "right" way to observe a holiday. What is a joyous tradition for one family might be a bore to someone else. Having the kind of holiday that is meaningful to you and your family is what matters.

5. **In a painful extended family, you may find it necessary for your own sanity to say "no" to family gatherings.** If you do make this choice, it will be easier if you can do so in a positive rather than a negative way. If you decide you simply can't join everyone at Aunt Dorothy's this year, don't sit home that day feeling guilty because you didn't go. And don't feel you need to explain to everyone why you are not going. Instead plan a special alternative with other family members or close friends. Then you can say, "We've decided not to go to Aunt Dorothy's this year because we are going on a wonderful ski trip." And you can enjoy a celebration shared with those you truly care about — folks you really want to spend time with.

6. **If your family has an annual hassle over "who do we spend the holidays with this year", it would help to work out in advance when to visit whom.** Plan to spread visits over the holiday season, rather than crowding them all into a few days. An early or belated celebration that is relaxed can be far more pleasant for everyone than a quick visit on the "right" day. Don't turn celebrations into hectic pit-stops, full of needless pressure. And avoid at all costs building up holiday guilt about not being all the other places you "should" be.

7. **Try planning some creative family time.** Making homemade gifts together can be fun for some families. Making gifts for nursing home or hospital patients can be rewarding, especially if you deliver them together. Perhaps you could help serve holiday dinner at a shelter or mission. Try something as simple as an evening walk to look at holiday displays. It might be possible to rent a sleigh for an outing you'll always remember. As part of your gift-giving, try a sharing time to talk about holiday memories or tell stories or share New Year's resolutions. Or give yourselves the gift of a special family vacation instead of the usual gift exchange.

   If your family isn't used to spending funtimes together, try some small steps first. You can't expect to wave a magic wand and turn everyone into a perfect picture of togetherness. But you can get everyone to try one activity that sounds like fun, and one shared experience will lead to the next.

8. **Give yourself permission to spend the holidays in ways that are important to you** — and extend that same permission to other family members. Maybe watching football on New Year's Day is as important to someone else as attending a church service is to you. Perhaps an evening at home alone would mean more to your spouse than attending an elaborate party. Maybe for teenagers, time with

close friends comes ahead of visits to relatives they rarely see

This doesn't mean you have to give up any attempts at family togetherness and let the holiday become just another day with everyone going their separate ways. But it is important to maintain some give and take. Make sure that, as you start to change holiday traditions, you don't turn right around and rigidly impose new ones of your own on others. It is important to agree as a family on which traditions are worth keeping and which ones lack meaning.

9. **Don't over-schedule.** Practice declining invitations that are "ought to", rather than "want to" occasions. For events such as office parties that are "musts" but not something you enjoy, try putting in a token appearance and leaving as soon as you can. Rather than crowding in many holiday events, choose one or two close nurturing friends and attend one special seasonal observance. Or just go to a movie or share a quiet dinner. Perhaps you could plan a "January Blahs" party for after the holidays instead of giving one at the height of the season when everyone is rushed. You don't need to turn into Scrooge and withdraw completely from holiday activities, but you can choose to participate only in the ones you enjoy.

10. **Try not to overbuy.** If you feel guilty because you don't give enough attention to your children, try giving them a gift of your time rather than expensive toys you can't afford. You could try a set of gift certificates — good for one of those outings you keep promising to do "some day", or for time to work on a particular project together or even just 10 minutes of uninterrupted listening. Try a gift of a game or a kit, along with a commitment to use it together. Be realistic — be careful not to go overboard and make promises it won't be possible to keep.

11. **If it makes you feel like a hypocrite, don't give gifts to family members you're emotionally "divorced" from or to business associates you don't care about.** In some cases, not giving a gift would cause awkwardness more uncomfortable than the hypocrisy of giving one. In this situation, try a card with an announcement that you're giving a donation to a charity in their name.

12. **Finally, give high priority to yourself — schedule some time alone.** This might be a retreat, a day at a spa, a professional massage or even just an hour in a bubble bath with a favorite book. This gift to yourself can be an important way of affirming that you care about your own needs.

    You might also share that same gift with others. You and your spouse or a friend could get together to make that time alone possible for one another.

    Regardless of the ways you choose to spend your holidays, there is one all-important observance. Very especially, plan for some time between you and your Higher Power. Make that a time to be aware of the ways you have gained strength. Make it time to be grateful for life, growth and connection.

This year give yourself a present. Plan your holiday season to be grounded in reality rather than unreal expectations. Make the child you give to this season be your own inner child. Make the holiday season a celebration of life and for life. And have a happy holy holiday.

What Can I Do?

Tools For Building a Coupleship

1. Focus on the positive aspects of the relationship.Whether you realize it or not, you do have the choice of highlighting the best parts of your spouse or you can focus solely on the parts that disappoint you. Pay attention and be aware of the small but significant ways your relationship sustains you. Many wonderful things about a spouse often go unnoticed and unappreciated.

2. Divide responsibility in a way that fits both of you. A certain number of chores have to be done — by someone. Decide who does what and do it. Try to allow maximum time to just be together. Problems arise when style and efforts clash. Work out the problems, rather than let them cause resentments. Do what each does best. Dividing work fairly is essential to a good relationship. But fairness sometimes needs to give way to thoughtfulness. That's the time that one chooses to do extra and give the partner some relief.

3. Know when it's important to compromise. So often people think that compromise means giving in or giving up. Yet compromise usually means that both sides win. In a successful partnership, neither partner balks or sets up insurmountable obstructions. Each partner's own individual needs are important, but in a coupleship partners also recognize the needs of the other. Couples generally find the best way to get each partner's needs met is through compromise.

4. Accept conflict as a necessary element in marriage. When two people decide to have an intimate relationship, they're going to live in each other's space. There will be inevitable conflict that will demand constant resolution. Each resolution will

increase intimacy. Many couples welcome conflict because they know that successful conflict resolution will bring about greater closeness.

5. **When non-resolvable conflicts occur, seek outside help.** Love needs maintenance, attention, discussion, scrutiny, adjustments, confrontation and work. Sometimes it's very difficult for the partners to be objective about a certain issue. When you get stuck and nothing seems to help, seek out a competent counselor and work through the problem. Each problem not resolved acts like a brick placed between two people. Enough bricks become a wall and the coupleship suffers.

6. **Let some things pass.** Not everything is worth a confrontation and it's sometimes wiser to let some things go by. If the partner is pretty great in many areas, it's simply not worthwhile to raise a fuss over a minor issue. Don't take each situation personally. Chalk up an unpleasant happening to a bad day, thoughtlessness or preoccupation with other things.

7. **Do not insist on instant resolution.** At times relatively quick resolutions of problems can take place. For example, a partner's bad temper after a traffic ticket may cause a blowup that can be handled with a little understanding or an apology. But serious problems, like whether to move to another city for the sake of a spouse's career, can't be resolved in a simple discussion. In such cases, indicate your commitment to finding an acceptable solution, and agree to take time to give the problem more thought and more discussion.

   In fact, a respite may be the wisest course. Many people think they have to talk everything out right away, but sometimes, it's better to wait. You may have to let it go for a while. "Good night" doesn't mean it's settled, just that you'll get back to it later.

8. **Stay focused on the now.** Stay with how you feel this minute. Don't become a collector of hurts — don't drag in past history or look for revenge. You'll simply block communication.

   Remove words like "always" and "never" from your vocabulary — as in "You're *never* home" or "You *always* spend too much money". The underlying message of such phrases is, "You're a flop as a human being" — a message not exactly designed to improve relations between you.

9. **Avoid blame.** When there's a dispute, forget who's right, who's wrong and whose fault it is. The odds are neither one of you is without sin, and blaming forces the other person to become defensive. You can't have winners and losers in a good coupleship. Both partners have to win.

   Name calling is out-of-bounds, too, and undermines respect. Ask yourself, "Do you want to hurt the other person or do you want to solve the problem?"

10. **Stick to one issue.** If you're mad because your mate left dirty dishes in the sink rather than loading them in the dishwasher, talk about that specifically — not the many flaws in his character. If you skip back and forth, you may evade the real point. But if you're honest, sincere and straight forward, you can discuss a single matter in five or ten minutes. Couples who talk over a simple problem for hours and hours or all weekend aren't really communicating. They may be using the simple problem as an indirect way of trying to talk about more serious issues. But because it's indirect, the communication is not effective.

11. **Stay with your own feelings.** Concentrate on them, not the other person's behavior. Talk in terms of "I feel", not "You did". Do it appropriately, however, not as an excuse to cut your partner down.

12. **Acknowledge a mate's anger.** Don't tell a mate, "You shouldn't be mad about that." We feel what we feel and such a statement simply fans the flame. Instead acknowledge the anger with, "I know how mad you are, but I didn't mean it that way."
13. **Go to bed together.** TV is an intimacy killer, and plenty of fights trace back to one spouse who wants to watch "Hill Street Blues" when the other is feeling romantic. Some people actually use TV as an excuse to avoid sex altogether.

    Even if sex isn't the issue, some couples rarely watch the same programs. Instead they spend evening after evening in separate rooms, watching different shows. They don't work things out because they're watching TV.

    If you feel rejected, a partner's attention to television only makes it worse. You soon get the feeling that TV is more important than you are. I don't advocate that you give up your favorite show. But television should not be used as a way of avoiding intimacy. Balance is needed. A sense of connection and closeness can get lost when there's a consistent pattern of separate television watching.
14. **Cuddle before going to sleep.** Kiss, hug or make a loving touch a "good night" ritual. Some couples do it instinctively. It's not sex that's so important, it's the loving gesture. Unfortunately many people live without it. They just share the same house.

Coupleship Checklist

So many things to learn, so many things to do. Are they working? I've put together a simple checklist so you may see how the coupleship is doing. My hunch is you already know. It feels great or it doesn't. Nevertheless, the checklist might help pinpoint certain areas that need some attention.

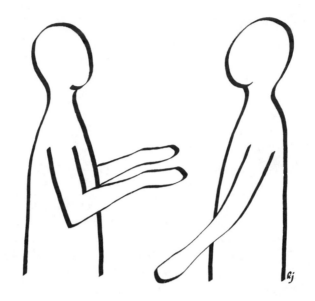

Do you love yourself enough to ask for what you need?

Check and discuss (true or false)

- ☐ We have a good time together, even if we're not doing something special
- ☐ I get excited knowing we are going to spend some time together
- ☐ I miss my mate when we are not together
- ☐ My partner is the person with whom I want to grow old
- ☐ When we are together, I feel a certain completeness and well-being

Discuss whether the characteristics of a satisfying coupleship apply to the two of you . . .

1. **You each accept yourself fully.** There is a basic self
   love and love for each other that you take time to
   nourish.
2. **You accept each other without trying to change
   each other.**
3. **You are both in touch with your feelings and share
   them with each other.**
4. **You are able to freely talk about your sexual
   wants, desires, thoughts and needs.**
5. **You cherish each other's body, beliefs, values,
   interests and accomplishments.** You validate
   yourself and each other.
6. **You present a union to family and friends.**
7. **You have clear boundaries** — established and
   protected by the two of you.
8. **You each protect yourself,** your health and your
   well-being and do what you can to help your mate.
9. **You are able to share your spiritual self** with your
   partner and are open to hearing about your
   partner's spiritual self. You respect each other's
   feelings and thoughts in this area.
10. **You are both willing to work** in whatever way that
    is necessary to enhance the coupleship. This
    includes seeking outside help.

Summary

Those capable of coupleship . . .

★ Have an outlook that is a couple's orientation toward shared experience

★ Give each other full and honest information

★ Trust each other

★ Take responsibility for self and are responsible to each other

★ Are loyally devoted to the other and have eliminated jealousy from their partnership

★ Are assertive, without being obnoxious, sarcastic and aggressive

★ Know how to fight fair and frequently

★ Are very affectionate

★ Are self and other accepting

★ Know how to discern what is important and what isn't

★ Have a sense of humor

★ Stick together in the hard or down times

★ Know how to play and laugh together

★ Are sexual with each other and maintain a sexually exclusive relationship

★ Know how to pray together

> *Intimates together in coupleship know how to be ever so close and still let the winds of heaven dance between them.*

____ NOTES AND REFERENCES ____

Foreword

George B. Leonard, "This Man and Woman Thing," *Look*, December 24, 1968.

This study comes from J.F. Cuber and Peggy B. Harnoff: *The Significant Americans*, New York: Appleton-Century-Crofts, 1965; mentioned in *Couples*, by Carlfred Broderick, New York: Simon and Schuster, 1979.

"Spirited": See my book *Choicemaking* for a discussion of Spirited and Spiritually Dead relationships. *Choicemaking*, by Sharon Wegscheider-Cruse, Pompano Beach, Florida: Health Communications, Inc., 1985.

Chapter One

"Touch": For a thorough discussion of the role of skin and the importance of body contact in relationships, see *Touching: The Human Significance of Skin* by Ashley Montagu, New York: Harper & Row, 1978. p. 2. He spells out the connection between touch and intimacy: "Touching, like being called by first name, is considered an act of intimacy, a privilege usually granted only to those of one's own class or status who one has allowed to pass across those social barriers which serve to exclude the unprivileged." Montagu points out that touching has limits. And much more than first-name-calling, touching "reduces social distance and often constitutes a declaration of intimacy. It is for this reason that it is so often regarded as an incursion upon one's privacy by those who resent such intrusions. By extension any accidental or unnecessary touching even from an intimate may be found annoying or unacceptable."

"The Winds of Heaven": from *The Book of Runes* by Ralph Blum, New York: St. Martin's Press, 1984.

Chapter Two

Couples by Anita Taylor and Robert Taylor, Washington, DC: Acropolis Books, 1978. Their definition of a couple: "A couple is any union of two persons which forms to fill mutual needs and which persists for a measurable period of time. The needs filled may be trivial or profound and the duration of the relationship may be fleeting or enduring."

Marriage Between Equals by Robert Seidenberg, Garden City, NY: Anchor/Doubleday, 1973.

Open Marriage by Neena O'Neill and George O'Neill, New York: M. Evans and Co, 1972. This book was written about a "new lifestyle for couples," a provocative examination of the traditional marriage contract, rewriting it with new guidelines for psychological commitment. The new lifestyle was one in which the partners worked on the relationship to enhance it, treated each other with respect as equals, and questioned traditional roles. It is one of the great ironies that the term 'open marriage' has come to be synonymous with the narcissistic gratification implied in the statement, 'You do your thing, and I'll do mine.' The O'Neills recognized that this attitude was destructive of relationships "Open marriage is looking at your life together as a cooperative venture, in which the needs of each can be fulfilled without an over-riding dependency that cripples the other's self-expression. Love can then be understood as a sharing of one another's independent growth rather than as a possessive curtailment of growth. Equality in open marriage is a state of mind, supported by respect and consideration for each other's wishes and needs . . . The difference between closed marriage and open marriage is the difference between coercion and choice."

In a later book, *The Marriage Premise,* Neena O'Neill commented on the "widespread misinterpretations" made of *Open Marriage:* "In describing our model for an ideal marriage of equality, George and I devoted the book to suggesting how couples might build a relationship of trust, intimacy and commitment through true sharing and caring. As an entirely optional consideration, not as an integral part of our model for an open marriage, we opened up the topic of outside relationships . . . We were thus surprised to see **open marriage** become a term, not for the new relationship of equality we had described, but for everything from a **sexually open** marriage to almost anything else . . . Like a Rorschach test, it mirrored the readers' perceptions, to say nothing of the perceptions of those who did not read it, but thought they knew what it was all about. It was most often misinterpreted as open sex, and so became a convenient label for everything from a non-caring, do-your-own-thing relationship to an intellectual justification for what people had been doing sexually all along, or wished they were doing . . . For all its applications, interpretations and misinterpretations, sexually open marriage is still one possibility — but only, and then only rarely, in the context of a marriage fully open in every other respect. We never suggested it was for everybody, and I do not suggest it now. For most people, sexual exclusivity is still a fundamental premise in marriage and a symbol of their loyalty to each other." *(The Marriage Premise* by Neena O'Neill, New York: M. Evans and Company, 1977.)

Royce Ellis Daniels poem, "Reminders" . . .

The Mirages of Marriage by William J. Lederer and Don D. Jackson, New York, W.W. Norton & Company, 1968.

Chapter Four

"High Monogamy: See "The End of Sex," by George Leonard, *Esquire,* December 1982.

"Two Sociologists": See "Sex As Work," by Lionel S. Lewis and Dennis Brissett in *Challenge of the Heart,* edited by John Welwood, Boston: Shambala, 1985.

"Kit Bag": See *Intimate Partners: Patterns in Love and Marriage* by Maggie Scarf, New York: Random House, 1987.

Chapter Five

"Boston Sociologist": See *Uncoupling: Turning Points in Intimate Relationships* by Diane Vaughan, New York: Oxford University Press, 1986.

"Maggie Scarf": From *Intimate Partners* by Maggie Scarf, New York: Random House, 1987.

"Life Cycle": See *Couples: The Art of Staying Together* by Anita Taylor and Robert Taylor, Washington, DC: Acropolis Books, 1978.

"Contact Sport": From *Couples* by Carlfred B. Broderick.

"Uncoupling": These comments appeared in an interview with Diane Vaughan in *People Weekly,* March 2, 1987.

Chapter Six

"Leo Buscaglia": Quoted in "Dr. Hug Will Uplift You," by Lynn Langway, with Janet Huck, in *Newsweek,* May 9, 1983.

Part II

"Viscott": Quotes from David Viscott in Part Two are taken from *How to Live With Another Person* by David Viscott, New York: Pocket Books, 1976.

_____ **Appendix** _____

The Coupleship
Intensive Program

_____

In the life of a couple there are special times when the relationship seems to need special attention. Such times may occur during the initial stage of couple formation *or* in early marriage — *or* during transitions with children, jobs, death in the family. Relationships may need special attention during times of unresolved disagreement and conflict or during prolonged hurt.

It has been my experience that in times of stress (*positive or negative*) there is a heightened potential for misunderstanding, emotional turmoil and feelings of rejection. Even the strongest of coupleships undergo complicated misunderstandings.

In my work with coupleship seminars and workshops I have learned:

   a) The majority of couples who seek help are able to get through even chronic turmoil, conflict and misunderstanding between partners. They find greater hope, commitment and joy as the result of

the opportunities to explore coupleship in depth
and to experiment with ways to enhance relationships.

b) There are some couples who should never have
come together in the first place, or who are clinging
to a relationship that has died. We often find one
person striving against overwhelming odds — and
with great cost in terms of physical and emotional
health — to hold a dead relationship together. In
these instances we help the partners see the obvious
reality of their unhappy alliance — which may result
in further helping the couple become able to
separate in the healthiest way possible.

At Onsite we offer five-day intensive workshops for
couples. The couples attending these five-day intensives can
be placed in roughly three categories:

- First, there's the coupleship where both partners have
  been active in their individual growth and self-
  awareness. They have acquired lots of tools for
  personal growth and now want to put them to work
  to enhance the relationship.
- There is another coupleship where neither partner
  has had personal growth experiences, nor have they
  learned communication or conflict resolution skills.
  Yet they are both open, eager to learn and willing to
  explore new ways of relating to each other.

Both of these types of couples work in special groups and
have a great chance of coming away from the five-day
intensive workshop with new, usable skills aimed at
enhancing intimacy, communication and commitment.

- The third type of couple is the most difficult to work
  with. The partners have a conflicted, estranged
  relationship and they come to the five-day intensives
  with great apprehension — mixed with fear, anger,
  frustration and hurt. This is the couple where one
  person has been working to hold the relationship

together and has developed some new ways of relating, while the other partner has been obstructive — openly resistant to change or finding subtle ways to sabotage the relationship.

In the five-day intensives, we find that the resistant partner is usually unwilling to participate fully — the commitment is just not there. However, a few of these couples do have a meaningful — and even dramatic — breakthrough and recommit to the relationship. They are able to accept feedback from the group about the status of their relationship and — for the first time — they are able to look at their relationship clearly and find areas of agreement about how they'd like to continue as a couple.

In the Onsite five-day intensive couples workshops we cover numerous topics, including intimacy, sexuality, the psychology of touch, values, communication, biochemistry of emotions, trust, play and conflict resolution. Couples spend time exploring how they came together, where they are now and how they would like their coupleship to be in the future.

Feedback from couples who have attended our workshops or similar couples groups indicates that it's very important to have the opportunity to share with other couples in a safe atmosphere. The five-day intensives provide enriching experiences for almost everyone, and for many couples the experience has been truly life-changing.

For more information about five-day intensive couples groups and other coupleship-building seminars, contact:

Onsite
2820 West Main
Rapid City, South Dakota 57702

Other Books By . . .

HEALTH COMMUNICATIONS, INC.

Enterprise Center
3201 Southwest 15th Street
Deerfield Beach, FL 33442
Phone: 800-851-9100

ADULT CHILDREN OF ALCOHOLICS
Janet Woititz
Over a year on The New York Times Best Seller list,this book is the primer on Adult Children of Alcoholics.
ISBN 0-932194-15-X   **$6.95**

STRUGGLE FOR INTIMACY
Janet Woititz
Another best seller, this book gives insightful advice on learning to love more fully.
ISBN 0-932194-25-7   **$6.95**

DAILY AFFIRMATIONS: For Adult Children of Alcoholics
Rokelle Lerner
These positive affirmations for every day of the year paint a mental picture of your life as you choose it to be.
ISBN 0-932194-27-3   **$6.95**

CHOICEMAKING: For Co-dependents, Adult Children and Spirituality Seekers — Sharon Wegscheider-Cruse
This useful book defines the problems and solves them in a positive way.
ISBN 0-932194-26-5   **$9.95**

LEARNING TO LOVE YOURSELF: Finding Your Self-Worth
Sharon Wegscheider-Cruse
"Self-worth is a choice, not a birthright", says the author as she shows us how we can choose positive self-esteem.
ISBN 0-932194-39-7   **$7.95**

LET GO AND GROW: Recovery for Adult Children
Robert Ackerman
An in-depth study of the different characteristics of adult children of alcoholics with guidelines for recovery.
ISBN 0-932194-51-6   **$8.95**

LOST IN THE SHUFFLE: The Co-dependent Reality
Robert Subby
A look at the unreal rules the co-dependent lives by and the way out of the dis-eased reality.
ISBN 0-932194-45-1   **$8.95**

Books from . . .
Health Communications

THIRTY-TWO ELEPHANT REMINDERS: A Book of Healthy Rules
Mary M. McKee
Concise advice by 32 wise elephants whose wit and good humor will also
be appearing in a 12-step calendar and greeting cards.
ISBN 0-932194-59-1 $3.95

BREAKING THE CYCLE OF ADDICTION: For Adult Children of Alcoholics
Patricia O'Gorman and Philip Oliver-Diaz
For parents who were raised in addicted families, this guide teaches you
about Breaking the Cycle of Addiction from *your* parents to your children.
Must reading for any parent.
ISBN 0-932194-37-0 $8.95

AFTER THE TEARS: Reclaiming The Personal Losses of Childhood
Jane Middelton-Moz and Lorie Dwinnel
Your lost childhood must be grieved in order for you to recapture your
self-worth and enjoyment of life. This book will show you how.
ISBN 0-932194-36-2 $7.95

ADULT CHILDREN OF ALCOHOLICS SYNDROME: From Discovery to Recovery
Wayne Kritsberg
Through the Family Integration System and foundations for healing the
wounds of an alcoholic-influenced childhood are laid in this important
book.
ISBN 0-932194-30-3 $7.95

OTHERWISE PERFECT: People and Their Problems with Weight
Mary S. Stuart and Lynnzy Orr
This book deals with all the varieties of eating disorders, from anorexia to
obesity, and how to cope sensibly and successfully.
ISBN 0-932194-57-5 $7.95

Orders must be prepaid by check, money order, MasterCard or Visa.
Purchase orders from agencies accepted (attach P.O. documentation)
for billing. Net 30 days.
    Minimum shipping/handling — $1.25 for orders less than $25. For
orders over $25, add 5% of total for shipping and handling. Florida
residents add 5% sales tax.